Richard Fiordo

Arguing in a Loud Whisper

A Civil Approach to Dispute Resolution

D0412192

VDM Verlag Dr. Müller

Impressum/Imprint (nur für Deutschland/ only for Germany)
Bibliografische Information der Deutschen Nationalbibliothek: Die Deutsche Nationalbibliothek
verzeichnet diese Publikation in der Deutschen Nationalbibliografie; detaillierte bibliografische
Daten sind im Internet über http://dnb.d-nb.de abrufbar.
Alle in diesem Buch genannten Marken und Produktnamen unterliegen warenzeichen-, marken-
oder patentrechtlichem Schutz bzw. sind Warenzeichen oder eingetragene Warenzeichen der
jeweiligen Inhaber. Die Wiedergabe von Marken, Produktnamen, Gebrauchsnamen,
Handelsnamen, Warenbezeichnungen u.s.w. in diesem Werk berechtigt auch ohne besondere
Kennzeichnung nicht zu der Annahme, dass solche Namen im Sinne der Warenzeichen- und
Markenschutzgesetzgebung als frei zu betrachten wären und daher von jedermann benutzt
werden dürften.

Coverbild: www.ingimage.com

Verlag: VDM Verlag Dr. Müller GmbH & Co. KG
Dudweiler Landstr. 99, 66123 Saarbrücken, Deutschland
Telefon +49 681 9100-698, Telefax +49 681 9100-988
Email: info@vdm-verlag.de

Herstellung in Deutschland:
Schaltungsdienst Lange o.H.G., Berlin
Books on Demand GmbH, Norderstedt
Reha GmbH, Saarbrücken
Amazon Distribution GmbH, Leipzig
ISBN: 978-3-639-32891-2

Imprint (only for USA, GB)
Bibliographic information published by the Deutsche Nationalbibliothek: The Deutsche
Nationalbibliothek lists this publication in the Deutsche Nationalbibliografie; detailed
bibliographic data are available in the Internet at http://dnb.d-nb.de.
Any brand names and product names mentioned in this book are subject to trademark, brand
or patent protection and are trademarks or registered trademarks of their respective holders. The
use of brand names, product names, common names, trade names, product descriptions etc.
even without a particular marking in this works is in no way to be construed to mean that such
names may be regarded as unrestricted in respect of trademark and brand protection legislation
and could thus be used by anyone.

Cover image: www.ingimage.com

Publisher: VDM Verlag Dr. Müller GmbH & Co. KG
Dudweiler Landstr. 99, 66123 Saarbrücken, Germany
Phone +49 681 9100-698, Fax +49 681 9100-988
Email: info@vdm-publishing.com

Printed in the U.S.A.
Printed in the U.K. by (see last page)
ISBN: 978-3-639-32891-2

ARGUING IN A LOUD WHISPER:
A CIVIL APPROACH TO DISPUTE RESOLUTION

TABLE OF CONTENTS

LESSON ONE

Perspectives on Argumentation

Lesson Objectives:

To provide an overview of argumentation and its use in this course

To discuss various perspectives on argumentation

To explain the role of dissent and consent, point and counterpoint in argumentation

To explain the role of resistance and context in argumentation

To relate argumentation to deliberation, discussion, debate, inquiry, and conversation

To relate argumentation to dialectics and rhetoric

To relate dialectics to conflict and conformity, division and unity

To present the mindful dialectic approach to argumentative communication

Overview

There is a time, place, and way to argue and a time, place, and way not to argue. This text on argumentation is set in a North American milieu and attempts to help you distinguish an optimal time, opportunity, and medium to engage others in sane, reasonable, and civil disagreement from times, opportunities, and media that fall short of being optimal. As an area of rhetorical discourse, perhaps best described as epistemic rhetoric, argumentation should be understood here to include a conditionally productive form and dynamic of communication on controversial matters. Freedom of speech and expression may battle daily against forces that aim to silence all but one partisan position. To be open to argumentation is to embrace questions that have not been asked as well as those that have been asked and have inadequate answers (Frankfort, 2005, p. 3). Our society is plagued by nonsense, claptrap, and humbug (pp. 1 & 5). Argumentation applied ethically has the potential to serve as an antidote to quackery and other manifestations of untruth. In other words, to argue with another in a context and manner acceptable and beneficial to both constitutes a rare privilege and honor. Argumentation constitutes a noble attempt in communication to boldly go where we have not gone before but to go there without hurting others. In this text, we trek through our differences together in a respectful and reasonable manner.

Argumentation as civil discourse should never be taken for granted; in fact, civil discourse is elevated and occurs too infrequently. In numerous contexts, reason and fairness may not be the ruling values. Reprisal may follow from voicing divergent viewpoints. Consequently, the choice to argue should be mindful. Arguers must decide that it is absolutely necessary to express disagreements in situations where negative results are likely. Since decision makers may not accept sound, valid, and good arguments, those who disagree must be mindful and careful of the consequences of voicing opposite views under circumstances inimical to differing points of views. Once the conditions have been noted, they may then proceed as they must.

An orienting, although not ultimate, definition of *argumentation* will be provided. The intention of this definition is to be as inclusive of other definitions of argumentation as possible. *Argumentation* is treated here as the study of the art and science of the theory, practice, and criticism of inquiry, advocacy, evidence, disagreement, and dispute resolution in communication through reasonable language and symbol use in communication contexts involving controversy with concord as a general goal. Broadly stated, *argumentation* is the study and practice of communicating reasonably under controversial circumstances.

Furthermore, in this text, argumentation is situated in the context of total quality management (TQM): a theory of progressive management whose aim is the overall improvement of its operation and the reduction of its risk. We borrow the notion of TQM and use it as an overall approach to argumentation that we describe as TQAM or total quality argumentation management (Dues & Brown, 2001, p. 45). Another principle we borrow from management theory is the orientation of *kaizen* or continuous quality improvement (CQI). CQI becomes CQAI or continuous quality argumentation improvement. We grant that no one can ever become too skilled in expressing disagreement, controversy, and dissent as well as harmony, agreement, and consent. We strive toward better argumentative standards, goals, performances, and outcomes. Our minimalist definition of *argumentation* is "communicating reasonably in controversy."

The democratic context of argumentation must be stressed here since it is assumed as the ground in which argumentation will flourish. While argumentation can exist under conditions that oppressively restrict free expression, it flourishes in an open communication setting that has democratic procedures in place and respected. For democracy to survive and flourish, *concordia discours* is the risky principle we must embrace. The concept of *concordia discors* (that is, discordant harmony or harmony in conflict) is seen as the essence of democracy and democratic functioning. *Concordia discors* constitutes the functional grounds for balancing disputing sides. With

4

argumentative criticism, this term may relate to the balancing of transparent communication with stifled communication which might include stonewalling, steamrolling, denial of requests, suppression of information, groupthink, oppression of opposition, prejudicial rewards, and discriminatory punishments - such as grievances, lawsuits, strikes, whistle-blowing, and boat-rocking (Conrad & Poole,2002; Miller, 2003; Dues & Brown, 2001; Shockley-Zalabak, 2000). For, we acknowledge, along with Foucault (Lotringer, 1989), as a power group blocks expression, the tensions for open expression are taking form as well simultaneously. In sum, an undemocratic goal of those with the resources, the power group, may be to control the outcome at the cost of freedom of expression. Their power strategy may work temporarily but not have long-range benefits; and, their undemocratic bullying risks boomerang effects, rebellion, non-compliance, non-cooperation, sabotage, and other forms of resistance to their anti-democratic and domineering maneuvers.

Judges play a critical role in weakening or strengthening democratic processes. Standards and criteria are commonly accepted as necessary parts of democratic systems. What is often lost in the critical democratic shuffle of factors is the important role of judges who determine the meaning of the criteria. Embedded in the critical system of standards is a critical system of judges. Judges, of course, vary in their decisions: whether film critics or court justices, adjudications vary. To have five judges in favor of a decision and four opposed is not unusual in law, nor is it mystifying to have five critics praise a film and four insult it. The judges and the system of judges might involve those who are usually fair and those who are usually biased as well as those having limited experience and those having extensive experience. The criteria may vary from being relatively unambiguous to highly ambiguous and from being relatively low to relatively high in bias. Overall, human beings can develop a system of judges and criteria that can be functional or dysfunctional; the function or dysfunction might be the consequences resulting from the use, misuse, or abuse of democratic procedures.

And, inarguably, the judges should be reasonable. Arguers should be open to diverse view yet willing to take a practical stance in light of the best information available when a decision is required. A positive attitude toward arguing and an inquiring attitude toward support for a thesis must be respected for optimal argumentation to unfold. Robert Frost, the American poet and four-time Pulitzer Prize winner, writes his poem "Fire and Ice" in a manner that embodies a wonderful and open attitude toward argumentation. He considers the pros and the cons of a vital issue. The poet probes the pros and cons of the end of the world while taking a poetic position on its outcome:

Some say the world will end in fire,

Some say in ice.

From what I've tasted of desire

I hold with those who favor fire.

But if it had to perish twice,

I think I know enough of hate

To say that for destruction ice

Is also great

And would suffice (Lathem, 1969, p. 220).

Frost favors the language of wisdom or the viewpoints on an issue from both or all sides of an issue and rejects the language of folly or the viewpoint on an issue from a single perspective. Clearly, Frost sides with the language of wisdom over that of folly (Lee, 1949). The author of this text sides with the language of wisdom as an operational norm and will later explain through a device he entitles the *mindful dialectic* that under rare circumstances, an excursion into the language of folly may be necessary for the greater good of a person, a community, or humanity in general.

The Semantics of "Arguing"

Student views and those of the general public on argumentation can be diverse, interesting, and inspirational. A selection of student views on arguing will be offered: 1) "I can't sit by and watch someone perpetuate ignorance just because no one else has the guts to say something"; 2) it "often takes more to walk away" from a verbal fight than to "get involved"; 3)"I feel that coming off as having a sensible, well thought out, and non-threatening point of view will make people more receptive to my line of reasoning"; 4) "I go into an argument knowing people will disagree with me, and that's okay with me; I enjoy having a different viewpoint from others because it is actually fun to argue with another even if neither of us give in"; 5)"I don't like to get into arguments that I don't think I'll win; however, although I'm not confrontational, because there are certain issues or people that cause me to get defensive, I have to let my feelings be known"; 6) I have a "very adversarial and confrontational approach to argumentation – an approach that wouldn't let people get a word in edgewise if I were engaging in a really heated argument"; 7) "I get very animated in voice, gesture, and body movement, others may take this to be a hostile and intimidating attack"; 8) "I avoid conflict and sometimes let another take complete control"; 9)"I love to argue because I love to be right and prove that I'm right; in other words, I like to bring out every single angle possible that would make the argument more interesting and slanted more in my direction"; 10) "Although speaking without thinking was a habit of mine and while I still have an opinion on almost every topic, I now try to base my opinions on facts and give others a chance to debate"; 11) "I used to think of arguing as a bad thing instead of an opportunity to voice my opinion and listen to the opinion of others"; 12) "I personally spend a great deal of my own time in the process of arguing or thinking of strategies to win arguments because arguing for me is exciting, entertaining, and most of all enjoyable; while I love hearing what others have to say and why their views are different from mine, what I really love is that small tinge of pride I feel when I know that I've won an argument; of course, losing is pure agony"; and, 13) "most people have no idea about how to argue with civility."

The statements from students on what it means to "argue" should alert us to the semantic reactions that are possible when we use the word. As an academic discipline, *argumentation* is a word used with analyzed care. The word has much descriptive and denotative value. In the everyday use of the term, the connotative meanings of the term may prevent us from using the word without causing bizarre and hostile semantic reactions. If we are among people who have a favorable association for the term *argumentation* and all of its derivative parts of speech, we may use the word with high descriptive accuracy and with favorable semantic associations. Two people with a respect for the term might get together happily to "argue" about a matter of concern to both. However, if we are among people with unfavorable associations for the term, we may have to use alternative terms and perhaps even avoid using any words that suggest that we are going to argue.

If those around us understand the word *argumentation* to mean communication that is confrontational and offensive, we should use other words to suggest a disagreement or difference of opinion is being offered. While we may not be willing to argue with another, we may be willing to express our point of view or question a viewpoint expressed or take issue with a statement that has been made. Although we will be arguing, we do not have to use the word to emphasize what we are doing. We can proceed with diplomacy and without using some form of the word *argue*. The semantic sensitivity of those with whom we communicate must be considered. With argumentation, we must be especially careful which words we use and do not use in communicating views we have that are different from those of another. Instead of saying, "Please let me <u>argue</u> my position on the issue," we might say, "Please let me give you my point of view on this matter." Instead of employing the semantics of "arguing," we might <u>argue</u> without using the word. With those hostile to the term, we are using an irreverent term. Consider semantic sensitivity pertaining to the word *argue* as part of the arguing you choose to do.

General Semantics Premises for Argumentation

As a sane and ethical mode of scientific, empirical, and experiential thinking and methods, the grounded and grounding principles of general semantics serve as sensibly critical premises from which to observe events, establish facts, filter inferences, and make judgments less prone to bias and nonsense. General semantics is seen here as the generalizing of the scientific attitude and method across all categories of learning and experience; that is, it is an attempt to be as grounded, sensible, and scientific as circumstances, conditions, and abilities allow across all disciplines – not just in one specialized category, such as biology or geology.

As a practical discipline that aims to get at the events behind and beyond the words, general semantics endorses the ways of ethically based critical thinking and scientific observation, testing, measurement, confirmation, and assessment as the ways of sanity (Hayakawa, 1990; Korzybski, 2000; Rapoport, 1950; Sawin, 1995; Levinson, 2002; Levinsion, 2007). This makes the principles of general semantics commonsensical, pragmatic, and verifiable in establishing what is real among symbol users anywhere. Selections of principles from general semantics that can be readily applied in argumentation as premises will be delivered now. Stories on general semantics written by Levinson (2007) inspired the formulation and organization of the following selections.

General semantics maintains that the world, swirling around us in perceivable and in atomic form, remains in constant flux. Whether we note or deny it, change, not permanence, constitutes the norm of material existence. Nothing stays the same. We are born, we age, and we die. While the Andes Mountains have a longer lifespan than a bamboo forest, change occurs in both. The Andes change at a relatively slower pace than the bamboo forest. Although neither is permanent, the Andes appear to be permanent while the bamboo forest seems perceivably fleeting. Change is caused. One or more things lead to one or more other things following with linked connections. Events have precedents and consequences. In short, change is inevitable and causation multifaceted (Fiordo, 2010a & 2010b).

Also, no two entities are the same: no two bamboo forests, no two mountain ranges, no two people, no two dolphins, no two falcons, and so on. Each creature has unique features and dynamics shared. When someone's son is sick or famous, it does not mean that person's daughter is sick or famous. No two entities are identical. Individual differences must be taken into account if sanity and

8

accuracy are to prevail. General semantics provides an inoculation against stereotyping and other forms of groundless generalizing. Being different and recognizing detailed differences constitutes a potential of being human. General semantics notes differences by indexing and dating individual entities: thus, Michael Jordan (1990) is not Michael Jordan (2010), and Michael Jordan (1) is not Michael Jordan (2).

Human beings abstract - select, extract, choose, underscore, highlight - features and dynamics from the world in all its materiality and complexity (Levinson, 2002). From the processes of nature, humans abstract or select aspects from the whole of the world they experience. The abstraction may occur with minimal or maximal bias. Whether done scientifically or egoistically, abstracting takes place. The abstracting leaves features and dynamics from the whole out. Human perception does not allow us to see atoms or internal processes, for example, in an organism. Blood is flowing, nerves are sending impulses, hearts are beating, molecules are changing, et cetera. Without scientific technologies, we do not perceive such changes although they are ongoing. Human perception allows us to see men or women walking or talking, dogs resting or barking, birds flying or chirping, et cetera.

Although abstracting allows marvelous human aspiration to become actuality, it can also become a problem because most humans have little or no awareness of its operation. When one person beholds another person or thing, abstracting is the norm. General semantics reminds us to look for what we are excluding in our abstraction from the reality we are beholding; it urges us to delay our reactions and make observations with alacrity. We benefit not only from what we see at first but from what we do not see at first. Since we cannot experience all things, we cannot report all things or say all that can be said about any one thing. Hence, we have to stay open to commentary on any person or thing. General semantics asks us to remember this by adding an actual or mental note through the terms *et cetera* or *etc*. Without the explicit or implicit "et cetera" concept, we may stop gathering information and close ourselves off to new and relevant information.

Abstracting also involves designations through language. Concrete nouns like *dog* and *car* contrast with abstract nouns like *democracy* and *fascism*. General semantics uses the analogy with a "ladder" of abstraction in which the concrete nouns are toward the ground and the abstract nouns toward the top of the ladder. The analogy of the ladder represents the upward and downward spirals of language: for example, from concrete nouns or words with low levels of abstraction to abstract nouns with high levels of abstraction. Language abstracts or highlights some features from the entity observed. If one has a particular dog named "Binx," that dog is different from all other dogs. The name of the particular dog "Binx" is an abstraction from the dog we perceive. However, once we classify

Binx as a "dog," the uniqueness of Binx is lost. We have gone up in abstracting from the phenomena of the special dog with the name "Binx." Every time we go up in abstraction, we lose more details from the actual phenomenon of Binx. So, when we classify Binx as an "animal" or a "being," we increase our levels of abstraction. Since abstraction can pose a problem created through the human ability to extract or select features and dynamics from phenomena, general semantics alerts us to this tendency to depart problematically on frequent occasions from the concrete and soar into the abstract (Fiordo, 1977).

One antidote general semantics provides rests in adopting an extensional orientation. Because words cannot completely describe anything, the extensional orientation guides us out of the heavens and toward earth and the observable. When we live in the world inside our heads, produced mostly through words, we can lose track of the world outside our heads. The extensional orientation helps us to stay in touch with the world we can directly observe or indirectly observe, especially through technological instruments like medical imaging or microscopes or telescopes. Indexing and dating are two ways to attain an extensional orientation. Operational and ostensible definitions are another, and there are more. When in doubt about high abstraction terms, we should be extensional. One way to extensionalize is to look to the world around us and point: for example, that white object in the sky at night is the "moon," and that bright object in the sky during the day is the "sun."

The extensional orientation has a counterpart – oftentimes unhealthy and problematic - in the intensional orientation. Both lie at opposite ends of a continuum. The person detached from verifying words through the senses and perception has an intensional orientation. In plain English terms, people with very heavy leanings toward an intensional orientation can be plagued with dangerous and unhealthy delusions or can at least demonstrate a lack of commonsense. People with very heavy leanings toward an extensional orientation tend to proceed with the sanity of observation and science. One important theme in general semantics is that the ways of science are the ways of sanity. Science in this context entails the sensible, reasonable, and ethical use of scientific method. An extensional orientation brings us to our senses: 1) sometimes through the direct observation of something like the rust-like appearance of steel in the Chicago Picasso in Daley Plaza in Chicago, Illinois or through the indirect observation of something like a tumor appearing in an MRI; 2) sometimes through the sophisticated method of a statistical scientific experiment to determine something like which of two medical treatments best treats a severe brain injury (Fiordo, 2010b).

The map-territory analogy of general semantics has overall value for communication and argumentation. Just as a map represents a territory and is not that territory, a word is like a map of a territory and represents it but is not it. The arbitrary link between a word and a referent becomes clear. As Abraham Lincoln once said, to call the tail of a mule a *leg* does not give the mule another leg. Maps can misrepresent territories, and the maps we rely on in our heads can be in error as well. For example, a traveler may accurately recall that Hiroshima and Nagasaki are two cities in Japan but situate them incorrectly in a mental map. Nagasaki is Kyushu south of Hiroshima which is in Honshu, but the traveler may switch the two in a mental map. After consulting an official map, the traveler will place each city in its proper geographical location. Faulty mental mapping occurs routinely in all areas of learning. One may wrongly think that Dante wrote the *Iliad* and Homer the *Inferno*: maps needing correction. Another may think President Eisenhower served as a Democrat: a map correction once again needed.

Most literal maps are static graphics, whether or not accurate. Some though are dynamic and change with the territory they are mapping like sonar and radar mapping. In language, maps tend to be static and biased like a Mercator projection of the earth. Distortion occurs in a Mercator projection of the earth. Greenland may look as large as South American when its actual size is close to that of Argentina. Subsequently, we must be careful with maps people use to represent territory. Those with intensional orientations incline themselves toward the map over the territory; those with extensional orientation incline themselves toward the territory over the map. When a conflict between the two occurs, the extensional person checks with the territory and corrects the map – a sanity of science. An intensional person denies the territory and adheres to the map – a sane to unsane act. Many people end up in mental institutions because of their tendency to be intensional ad absurdum. The general semantics preventive prescription is to discipline oneself to be extensional and direct oneself via the territory rather than the map when the two conflict (Fiordo, 2010a & 2010b).

Favoring empirical observation, commonsense, and scientific methods, general semantics prefers reports over inferences and judgments. Inferences and judgments must be respected but approached with scrutiny. Reports form the basic unit of establishing fact from observation or from the observations of others. Reports are statements of events or facts – statements that can be verified through observation: for example, "Badwater Basin is in Death Valley National Part." A visit to Death Valley would verify the existence of Badwater Basin. Inferences are interpretations of events or facts – statements about the unknown made on the basis of what is known. Many inferences can follow from a report. From the following report, two inferences will be noted. A person reports: "An NYPD police car is heading north on Broadway past the fashion district with the lights flashing and the siren sounding." Two inferences might be: 1) "The NYPD must be responding to a terrorist threat"; 2) "The NYPD must be chasing someone in a stolen care." Judgments are statements that favor one evaluation over another. For example, with the NYPD inference, a judgment might be: "The NYPD is the finest law enforcement agency in the country." However, while the report of the NYPD police car is headed north on Broadway may be correct, the police car might be stolen and driven by a criminal trying to escape the law. Inferences must be scrutinized.

Of course, there are many other facts followed by inferences: Stonehenge, the Shroud of Turin, the Mayan Pyramids, etc. In televised crime dramas like *Law and Order* and *CSI*, a repeating scene involves a corpse being found but the cause of the death is unknown. So, the story begins with the fact of the dead body and continues with statements about the unknown made on the basis of the dead body. Eventually, by finding and evaluating evidence, investigators discard invalid inferences, select valid ones, and prosecute the villain. Most people do not separate reports from inferences and judgments. Consequently, confusion replaces understanding with errors entering about the mapping of reality. Consequences follow from faulty assumptions about inferences or judgments being facts. Sanity follows from distinguishing inferences and judgments from facts. Argumentation becomes sensible when care is taken to delineate the differences expressed through language that forms reports, inferences, and judgments.

General semantics advocates a multi-valued logic over a two-valued logic (Hayakawa, 1990). Even a three-valued logic constitutes a better map of events than a two-valued logic. Although there are suitable contexts for a two-valued logic, a three-valued logic or multi-valued logic is closer to fact in most natural settings. A two-valued logic would give two alternatives: for example, true and false, right and wrong, hot and cold, good and bad, etc. A three-valued logic would allow a third value to be an option: for example, true and false and indeterminate, hot and cold and tepid, etc. A multi-valued logic deals with degrees. The degrees might be scaled and range from zero to 10, zero to a 100, or zero to infinity: for example, [true-1-2-3-N-false], [good-1-2-3-N-bad], etc. In short, going beyond two-valued logic, which can be a form of either-or thinking, can benefit communication and argumentation.

Time-binding is the last general semantics principle to serve us here as a premise for argumentation. Time-binding is the human capability and action of linking through language and symbol systems over time with former generations. Through the uniquely human time-binding, we learn to survive in the present from others from the past what to do in the future (Sawin, 1995). Optimally and optimistically, we learn the best from the past and carry ourselves forward from it; we leave the worst from the past. On the light side, time-binding allows humanity to connect with the scientific, artistic, literary, religious, political, medical, and other benign giants from the past. On the dark side, time-binding allows us to connect with malevolent giants from the past. With time-binding as a premise, argumentation benefits from lineage. Determining who is being honored by words and action, a humane arguer can build a case to reject malignant ties and embrace beneficent ties (Sawin, 1995).

Although but a selection has been provided here, additional general semantics premises are available to benefit someone considering argumentation. For an elaborated account of general semantics principles, please see Sawin's (1995) *Thinking and Living Skills: General Semantics for Critical Thinking.*

Argumentation Premises

Argumentation, as we use the term formally, investigates every use of language and symbols that addresses disagreements, conflicts, disputes, and controversies. Argumentation applies to the ethical and unethical use of language, reasoning, evidence, and nonverbal communication to present a view. We also distinguish that the dimension of argumentation that interests us most is the auspicious, efficient, reasonable, and humane use of communication to deal with conflict. Similar to Willard (1989), we see argumentation as being primarily a social phenomenon and secondarily as being a prescription for winning arguments. Argumentation therefore involves reason-giving as a social and interpersonal communicative activity.

Although argumentation does not have to be used in a democratic setting, for our purposes, argumentation is treated primarily in a democratic context. Subsequently, principles from parliamentary practice are respected and urged. Although any number of parliamentary authorities would suit our democratic contexts, Sturgis (1993) will serve us since this authority mollifies procedures in complex sources that may lead to parliamentary rules subverting parliamentary principles of democracy (p. xxiii). The principles of parliamentary law constitute our main concern for the creation of conditions conducive to fair and favorable argumentation to prevail.

The principles of parliamentary law relevant to our purposes follow: (1) The aim of parliamentary procedure is to facilitate business transactions and promote cooperation and harmony; (2) All members have equal rights, privileges, and obligations; (3) The majority vote rules; (4) Minority rights must be protected; (5) All members have the right to a full and free discussion of each

13

proposition presented for decision; (6) All members have the right to know the meaning of the question before the assembly and what its effect will be; and (7) all meetings must proceed with fairness and good faith (Ibid, pp. 7-10).

When these conditions prevail in a democratic setting, the odds of argumentation proceeding reasonably and sanely improve radically. When we proceed with a functional parliamentary authority that is utilized ethically, parliamentary procedure will likely help members accomplish their goals. Parliamentary procedure should not be used to "awe, entangle, or confound the uninitiated." Technical rules should be used "only to the extent necessary to observe the law, to expedite business, to avoid confusion, and to protect the rights of members" (Ibid, p. 7). With rights and duties for all members, the presiding officer has the responsibility to be "strictly impartial" and to "act promptly to protect the equality of members." After a vote, the decision is announced. The majority decision becomes the "decision of every member of the organization," and it is the "duty of every member to accept and to abide by this decision." As for minorities, it is the right of the minority through persuasion to change the will of the majority; for, the "minority of today is frequently the majority of tomorrow" (pp. 8-9).

Furthermore, every member of an assembly has the "right to speak freely without interruption or interference provided the rules are observed." That all members have the right to say what they wish is "as important as their right to vote." When it comes to understanding and comprehension, all motions and their effects should be clearly explained. All members have the right to request information on any motion they do not understand so that they may vote intelligently." Finally, trust, fairness, and good faith must prevail. What threatens these must be contained: namely, "trickery, overemphasis on minor technicalities, dilatory tactics, indulgence in personalities, and railroading" (p. 9). In short, the "good faith of the group" outweighs a "particular detail of procedure." The effectiveness and existence of a group are often "destroyed if its officers or members condone unfairness or lack of good faith" (p. 10).

Two practical democratic rules and rights will be detailed: voting and deliberation. Members of a democratic organization have the right to elect officers and decide on propositions. The right to a vote is a right to a voice in "determining the will of an assembly." Voting is the "most fundamental right of a member." Once taken, a vote constitutes a "formal expression of the will of the assembly" (p.133). Most methods of voting reveal who is voting and how that member is voting. Voting by ballot is the only exception and will be explained briefly. How members vote remains secret, and the secrecy is protected. If the secrecy is violated and the voter is identified, the vote becomes invalidated. A secret ballot vote is "usually required in elections and frequently in voting on important proposals." To safeguard the sanctity of the ballot vote, the "presiding officer should give careful instructions as to how the members should prepare their ballots" (pp. 135-136).

The second rule and right to be developed involves what Sturgis calls a motion for "informal consideration" and is used to deliberate productively on a proposition during a debate. The presiding officer has to control and expedite debate. If features of an issue are being overlooked, the presiding officer may stimulate discussion of those points to "contribute to a clear understanding of the motion and its effects" (p. 118). Sometimes, it is beneficial to the assembly to have the "discussion of a problem *precede* the proposal of a motion" so that the wording can be worked out intelligently and without formal procedures being allowed to inhibit the deliberative effort of the group. A motion to consider a motion informally permits a group to discuss openly, productively, and informally a potential motion rather than offering a poorly articulated actual motion formally. Instead of referring a motion to a committee, the motion for informal consideration handles the concern immediately. Once the motion for informal consideration has been made and voted in, the problem may be discussed until the problem is clarified. Then, a motion is made and this "motion automatically terminates the informal discussion, and the motion is considered and voted on under the regular rules of debate." If no clarification and agreement on the problem occurs, "informal discussion may be terminated by a motion to end the informal discussion" (pp.120-121).

What we have been discussing with respect to parliamentary law suggests a civility about making decisions in groups. Making decisions in general with civility will now be addressed. For argumentation to proceed without harshness (or with harshness only by default after all avenues have been exhausted), as a matter of wisdom and prudence, civility should reign supreme in argumentative dealings. Forni (2002, p. xi) tells us that he wants to persuade us to make "civility a central concern in our lives." Forni proposes that as a society, the US should examine a code of civil conduct based on "respect, restraint, and responsibility" (p. 5). In addition, since to a significant degree, "life is what our relationships make it," civility permits us to relate to others successfully (p. 6).

Among the behaviors embodying civility that Forni lists, several are conspicuously germane to argumentative communication. He suggests that we lower our voices whenever our raised voices may threaten or interfere with the tranquility of others, acknowledge a newcomer to a communicative interaction, listen to "understand and help," respect differences in others, react with "restraint to a challenge," own up to our mistakes, refuse to join others in "malicious gossip," to disagree with "poise," to yield graciously when we lose an argument (p. 9). In short, to be civil we behave in a manner that is considerate of others. When we are civil to others, we expect to be treated with civility in return. By being civil to you, I appeal to your civility and urge you to be civil to me. Thus, civility involves the "applying of gentle force with the goal that everybody be a winner in the delicate game of the social exchange" (pp. 26-27). Forni advises further that we "rediscover the teaching of civility and good manners" to improve everyone's quality of life. Since the manner in which we interact with others is crucial in social life, being civil should improve our quality of life. If we improve the quality of our communication, we improve the quality of our lives. We create the conditions for a "saner, more meaningful, healthier, and happier life" (p. 184). Obviously for argumentative communication, communication that involves conflict escalation and resolution, the practice of civility is rarely an option.

Invitational Grounds for Argumentation

With respect to orientation and strategy, argumentation, as dealt with from our perspective, draws from the invitational rhetoric of Foss and Foss (2003). Rhetoric involves discourse used for diverse practical social purposes. Rhetoric in this sense includes argumentation. The invitational rhetoric serves as the basis also for the mindful dialectic discussed later. In brief, the mindful dialectic involves our conscious choice to argue and to argue well once we decide to do so. We believe that in an overwhelming majority of cases, we should invite listeners to listen and transform themselves rather than conquer them with our so-called and erroneously conceived irrefutable logic. While Hikins (1996, pp.70-71) comments reasonably on possible limitations to this feminist perspective on rhetoric and argumentation and calls attention additionally to the problem of a Eurocentric tendency in rhetorical and argumentation theory, the dialogical utility of the invitational rhetoric causes us to use it here as a primary and practical humane orientation.

We also note that Asian, religious, and psychotherapeutic sources also utilize rhetorical and argumentative concepts that are dialogical and invitational: that is, that respect the listener as an equal and occasionally as a superior. While notions of argumentation from Asian, religious, and psychotherapeutic sources are mentioned here, they will be detailed in later articles. Such contributions as those from Buddhist, Daoist, and Zen Asiatic sources, Judeo-Christian and Islamic sources, and rational-emotive and integrity psychotherapy will not be covered in this writing. Any argumentation therapy methods, in other words, are not elaborated here. Rather, we summarize a feminist rendition of the invitational rhetoric as advanced by Foss and Foss since this perspective has already been elaborated and is timely and relevant to our objectives. We cover the feminist perspective on invitational rhetoric noting that Asian and other sources will be explained in a later article, and feminist writers should acknowledge and integrate Asian and other sources into their own theorizing on rhetoric and argumentation.

To illustrate this link with Asian thought to be developed later, writing on zen, Ruben Habito (2005), a native of the Phillipines and native speaker of Tagalog who teachers at Southern Methodist University, presents a rhetorical orientation that is even gentler than that of the invitational rhetoric. Viewing the teacher of zen as a midwife, Habito quotes a Zen proverb from Japan and praises its usefulness and kindness: *"Kuru mono wo kobamazu, saru mono wo owazu"* or "Not refusing those who come, not pursuing those who go" (www.mkzc.org/Ruben_Articles.html). In addition, the mission statement of the Maria Kannon Zen Center, which is a non-profit corporation offering a setting for "people of various backgrounds and faith traditions to practice Zen," includes the center's primary commitment to "offer people an opportunity to practice Zen mediation as well as promote an ecumenical haven of diverse meditation forms for practioners" (www.mkzc.org/About.html). To "offer an opportunity" constitutes language, as mentioned above, that is less demanding than the already gentle language of a rhetoric that invites transformations. This incipient theory of rhetoric places the locus of choice with the person welcomed upon arrival and perhaps invited as well. In discussing the Dharma, Habito actually uses the word "invitation" and its forms in his discourse on Zen study and experience: 1) Because "everything is impermanent, the invitation of the Awakened One is to live the fullness of this fleeting moment, just as it is"; 2) "So we are invited not just to look for the 'sweets' of the moment." There are also sour, bitter, and different kinds of tastes present. The are "all treasures that we are invited to taste in our life" (www.mkzc.org/sarana2.htm). And, of course, much more pertains to the communication methods of the Ch'an and Zen intuitive sects of Buddhism (Hopfe and Woodward, 2001, pp. 139-141) and will be explained elsewhere.

Invitational rhetoric, and argumentation which is a part of rhetoric, is a "form of communication designed to generate genuine understanding among individuals who hold different perspectives." Invitational rhetoric is rooted in five assumptions: "(1) the purpose of communicating is to gain understanding; (2) the speaker and the audience are equal; (3) different perspectives constitute valuable resources; (4) change happens when people choose to change themselves; and, (5) all participants are willing to be changed by the interaction" (pp. 9-10). As for personal change happening by choice, Foss and Foss quote Sally Gearhart, who is a rhetoric theorist, on turning an egg into a chicken. If the conditions are right, an egg hatches into a chicken. In contrast, a stone will under no conditions hatch into a chicken, no matter what the conditions. The egg has the potential to become transformed into a chicken, not the stone (p. 13). We will add that the chicken and stone analogies are valid unless we change the meaning of the word "stone" and cleverly convert the stone into a carving of a chicken. But then, we violate language and reason. When we make transformation possible, we respect the choices of others listening to us and communicating with us.

Using the invitational rhetoric as a communication guide, we might choose to argue to gain understanding by respecting one another as equals and listening to different points of view. We allow change to happen to one another internally by insuring that all communicators are open to change through the argumentative transactions. If these conditions prevail, we may argue humanely and effectively. In fact, we may decide to argue with others only when these conditions are present or can be created. Otherwise, we may conduct a monolog believing it is a dialog. We may be working hard at trying to hatch a stone!

Adapting the invitational rhetoric for general purposes seems wise in order to argue effectively. Understanding is no easy goal to accomplish. A broad range of social contexts are thus more likely to be respected in our multicultural society. Since life circumstances are usually more complex than our understanding of these circumstances, we may circumstantially integrate the invitational rhetoric into so-called domineering forms of argumentation. Such actions are recommended here only as adjustments to especially restrictive situations. Invitational rhetoric derives from the idea of an invitation which is the "request for the presence or participation of someone." To issue an invitation, we "ask someone to come somewhere or to engage in some activity" with us. The goal of invitational rhetoric is to reach understanding by sharing our experience through words. The objective is "not to win or prove superiority but to clarify ideas – to achieve understanding for all participants involved in the interaction." Invitational rhetoric aims to reduce the judgmental and adversarial framework for transactions with its emphasis on understanding (pp. 6-7).

While other modes of communication available to us – namely, conquest, conversion, benevolent, and advisory modes (Foss and Foss, 2003, p.7), our inclination in selecting a mode is frequently to default to the legitimate but limited modes of conquest through advisory rhetoric. Conquest rhetoric would be the highest level of default and advisory the lowest. Foss and Foss call these default modes to emphasize their theoretical and ethical inferiority to invitational rhetoric while crediting these modes with their legitimate and limited special functions pertaining to winning narrowly defined. Because we are disproportionately awarded in American society for adhering especially to the conquest and conversion modes, their value must be conceded yet discounted.

18

In other words, while conquest rhetoric has "winning as its goal," conversion rhetoric is "communication designed to change other' perspectives on an issue or to change how they behave in some way." The other modes entail benevolent rhetoric which aims to "provide assistance to individuals out of a genuine desire to make their lives better" and advisory rhetoric which tries to "provide requested assistance" (pp. 5-7). The habitual selection of conquest and conversion rhetoric by default produces in us adversarial positions that lead to verbal battles of right and wrong (p. 7). Figuratively speaking, we fight rather than talk, choose warfare over peace, turn to verbal violence before verbal inquiry, and select ego-centered expression over shared meaning. Understanding through communication may at best be incidental. So, by defaulting to alternative modes of argumentation only when circumstances demand it, we can base our argumentative communication on the more civil form of an invitational norm of rhetoric.

Two significant features of the invitational rhetoric include these options: (1) disengaging from the default modes of conquest and conversion and (2) formulating a response within a new framework. With disengagement, we might decide to "walk away from an encounter rather than continue a negative interaction." Clearly, this is a viable option and one that should be decided upon routinely and promptly. With formulating an alternative response, we might find a way to form creatively an invitational response to the default mode – especially those of conquest and conversion. Hence, we choose to communicate in a different framework and to engage in communication that fosters understanding by arguing indirectly with someone's viewpoint or by addressing some other viewpoint rather than the one being presented (pp. 44-45). Again, these are alternate approaches to the complexity of argumentation and its consequences.

Imperative and Manipulative Grounds for Rhetorical and Argumentation Discourse

Gutenberg (2007) adds a fundamental distinction to argumentation. In discussing his epistemic rhetoric which involves the "intentionality of speech actions," we can apply his ideas on rhetoric to argumentation. At least two argumentative (or convictive rhetorical) modes from Gutenberg can be discussed: namely, the manipulative (which short-circuits thinking to "provoke action-by-reflex") and the imperative (which "means the suppression of contradiction by verbal coercion with physical violence pending"). Manipulative argumentation might include commercials and political propaganda while imperative argumentation entails the proclamations of authoritarian, totalitarian, and centralized states and organizations. In contrast to argumentation functioning to convince audiences that have choices in democratic contexts, Gutenberg sets forth imperative and manipulative modes of argumentation designed to get results without having the goal of convincing an audience. Conviction is not needed in authoritarian contexts. Giving and taking orders in authoritarian organizations or totalitarian societies are more typical of what he sees as argumentative rhetoric since it does not aim to convince an audience of some point of view since choice is not an option. The audience must obey and comply.

Imperative and manipulative discourse thus involves language used to direct behavior without choice being a part of the equation and so without having the goal of convincing an audience. Gutenberg sees manipulative and imperative discourse as one-way argumentation: a case is presented and the audience accepts it or suffers negative consequences pertaining to their noncompliance. He locates such one-way manipulative argumentation in "private and everyday communication, such as selling from door-to-door, telemarketing) and such one-way imperative argumentation in "classroom communication and public administrative."

To assess imperative and manipulative discourse, Gutenberg suggests criticism that "aims at uncovering elements of manipulative and imperative rhetoric to improve convictive [that is, convincing] communication, be it in public or private, in institutions or organizations, for factually or personally oriented forms." Imperative and manipulative argumentation can be identified through their unilateral intention and their way of hindering an audience's freedom to choose. Manipulative discourse tries to block the free choice and thinking of an audience and operates as a perversion of two-sided or many-sided argumentation by providing spurious arguments in support of a prejudicial position. Imperative discourse does not have to bother as much with the audience as manipulative discourse does, for it may ignore the feelings and preferences of an audience. If imperative discourse considers the audience at all, it might be "only to such a degree as necessary for threat and blackmail." Imperative discourse, in short, is "power disguised in speech" and thus "fakes public address and group discussion." Nonetheless, imperative discourse "hardly deludes anybody, except perhaps the speaker" using the imperative mode. Imperative discourse overrides reciprocal and open communication through the "immanent threat of physical coercion when words fail."

Imperative and manipulative discourse thus serves, according to Gutenberg, as the counterpart to democratic discourse. To perform astute argumentative and rhetorical criticism, it is "important to look for tendencies of manipulative and imperative rhetoric in everyday life: in the pulpit, at school, in the public service, media, organizations, in political parties and public gatherings, and in constitutional assemblies." Both imperative and manipulative forms of discourse "would prefer no rhetoric at all on the addressee's part." Rather, each would "prefer a smoothly performing automatism of reaction and obedience." Language is used strategically in democratic contexts. In democratic contexts, rhetoric and argumentation have the potential to flourish. Language is used strategically in authoritarian contexts too. However, rhetoric and argumentation lose their potential to flourish and may be voiced only to be muted by intimidation and violence. Gutenberg therefore guides us in the recognition of a context ranging from democratic to authoritarian for generating and criticizing argumentative messages.

Diverse Contributions to Argumentation

Our approach to the study, theory, and pedagogy of argumentation includes traditional parameters but goes well beyond traditional boundaries for this subject. Logic, rhetoric, advocacy, persuasion, and debate all contribute to argumentation as presented here. Yet, more than other writings on argumentation, we elicit contributions from a number of ancient and modern disciplines. These include in general terms: human relations, dialectics, ethics, psychology, psychotherapy, psychopathology, conflict theory, conflict resolution, mediation, arbitration, bargaining, negotiation, deliberation, military theory, martial arts practice, parliamentary procedure, dialogical philosophy, dramaturgical theory, semantics, language analysis, feminism, and others.

Viewing argumentation broadly as expressed differences of opinion, what is emphasized are these contributing disciplines: (1) psychology (especially Albert Ellis' rational-emotive therapy); (2) dialectics (especially forms of deliberation noting hegemony and respecting human relations principles); (3) epistemology (especially methods for establishing evidence and reasoning); (4) conflict theory (especially procedures for managing hostilities); and, (5) feminism (especially the invitational rhetoric generated by Foss and Foss. In short, we respect the modern and ancient sources of traditional argumentation that flows from ancient rhetoric to modern forensics. However, while respecting these stalwart contributions, we expand the base and the height of the argumentative pyramid for use in diverse contexts in a rapidly diversifying world: a world diversifying methodologically, culturally, and technologically in its modes and manners of communication and argumentation.

Argumentation for our purposes covers its general and informal contexts more than its special and formal contexts; that is, we study how argumentation operates in everyday life as well as how it operates in court and public debate. Three graphic continua illustrate the relationships:

General and Informal - - - - - Special and Formal
Daily Life- - - - - Public Life
Everyday Conversations- - - - - Public Communication
Organizational Settings - - - - - Social Settings

Tempered by reason, truth, and practicality, open and free discussion is encouraged in our approach to argumentation. Although we urge disputants to communicate, we ask disputants and communicators to be on the alert for others and themselves becoming a contentious, offensive, contrary, know-it-all, and yappy communicator. We lightheartedly refer to this communicative response by the acronym of "COCKY." We support a person becoming COCKY only in response to special circumstances that are uncommonly demanding. So, usually, we should strive to be anything but COCKY. On rare and necessary occasions, we may have to become, for the sake of ourselves and others, COCKY: to implement humane ends, to pursue decent interests, and to protect rights and well-being through unconventional means. We must, as circumstances demand and humane decency requires, be open to think outside the box – that is, to practice divergent thinking. When we decide to clash over ideological or material issues, we must proceed with wisdom. A friendly version of this weighty principle is voiced in the song entitled "The Gambler" by Kenny Rogers: We have to "know when to hold them, know when to fold them, know when to walk away, and know when to run." If we incline ourselves toward avoiding clash routinely or toward clashing routinely, our beneficial effectiveness when arguing may be minimal or may even boomerang on us (Hocker & Wilmot, 1985).

When arguing (that is, expressing disagreement preferably, when possible, in a civil and reasonable manner), we must decide when the argumentative circumstances require transformers, fighters, lovers, dancers, explorers, or roles yet to be invented to yield the best results for all. An easy way to remember this is though several continua:

advocacy - - - - - inquiry
conquest - - - - - transformation
persuasion - - - - - understanding

At one extreme we advocate, conquer, and persuade like promoters or lawyers; and, at the other extreme, we inquire, transform, and understand like researchers and scientists. Between these extremes is where we are likely to find ourselves arguing much of the time.

Hegemony in Argumentation

West and Turner (2004, p. 366) define *hegemony* as the "influence, power, or dominance of one social group over another." Of course, hegemony works through the perpetuation of an ideology through discourse (Vande Berg, Wenner, & Gronbeck, 2004, p. 296). Our notion of hegemony derives primarily from Antonio Gramsci (1971). Gramsci held that the ruling elite utilize hegemony to gain consent from the remainder of society. Hegemony operates through a balanced blend of coercion (or force) and consent with force appearing to be based on a majority societal decision (p. 80). He grounded his concept of hegemony on Marx's idea of false consciousness: "a state in which individuals become unaware of the domination in their lives." Gramsci maintained that publics become exploited by the very system they endorse. Dominant social groups and individuals representing these groups manage to shepherd people into complacency largely through consent more than through coercion. People give consent when they receive enough freedom, material wealth, and so on. In short, people eventually support tacitly the dominant ideology of their culture (West & Turner, 2004, p. 366). From the perspective of John Fiske quoted in Vande Berg, Wenner, and Gronbeck (2004, p. 296), through ideology mediated by way of discourse, hegemony tends to "create common sense out of dominant sense."

Hegemony, in a society as complex and pluralistic as that of the US, may struggle and compete through the ideology of its discourse to oppose the dominant forces. Hegemony then gives rise to counter-hegemony. Audiences need not be duped always into accepting everything those in positions of domination present; they need not be willing, compliant, and submissive to a ruling authority or power. In counter-hegemony, people recognize their consent and do something about it. Muted voices become heard (West & Turner, 2004, pp.368-369). Also, hegemonic complicity, or the accepting of certain power relations as normal or natural, is opposed. The existing social order and its maintenance through voluntary compliance is challenged (Vande Berg, Wenner, & Gronbeck, 2004, p. 398). Thus, argumentation in a democratic society draws its energies from ideologies that are both hegemonic and counter-hegemonic. Through argumentative discourse, we struggle to maintain or change: that is, we participate in the dialectics of ideology and power.

Power and resistance and its context are pivotal concepts and realities in argumentative communication. Who might oppose whom with how much force and how many resources with what effect in any given context moderates the power of argumentative efforts. If resistance to an idea or position can be imagined (or observed) to produce tremendous opposition or indifference from those receiving the message, an arguer may decide to modify the message resulting in high tensions or low support. A case may be strengthened rigorously, made at another time, with other than the originally intended message receivers, using a different medium of communication, abandoned altogether, or modified considerably to suit the latitude of acceptance available at the time the message is transacted. To think of conflict and argumentation without thinking of resistance to ideas and positions would disadvantage the arguers irreparably. An estimate of resistance must be considered early in the advancement of a thesis or the probing of an investigation. If little resistance is anticipated and encountered, an arguer may proceed with reasonable boldness. If extensive resistance is anticipated and encountered, an arguer must proceed with a careful and powerful case – if a decision to proceed is made. Resistance factors must and should be noted and respected in preparing for or participating in argumentative conflict.

Types of power can be seen as constituting a sizable portion of resistance in any argumentative situation. While circumstances themselves – natural disasters plaguing a social group to telecommunications being absent in a community – can foil the advancement of an idea, our focus here will be on various types of social and human power that can create a barricade and opposition to building a case or sharing a new idea. Power bases, or the influence someone or some group has over others as a result of their dependency on some person or group (Shockley-Zalabak, 2001), must be assessed. Frequently used categories for power bases include: legitimate, reward, coercive, referent, expert, and connection power (p. 252). The power bases of those who oppose us must be examined to determine whether we should proceed with argumentation or how we should proceed to bring about our ends.

Legitimate power surfaces from the "positions, titles, or roles people occupy." Supervisors in particular may have this power. Reward power comes from someone's "control and distribution of tangible and intangible reward sources." Parents and teachers may have this power. Coercive power includes "sanctions or punishments" within someone's control. Coercive power enables someone to "punish for not complying with influence attempts." Supervisors, parents, and teachers may have this power. Referent power results from people identifying with someone as a mentor, leader, or guru. This form of power is assigned to some person or group by others. Expert power emerges from what some person or group knows authoritatively and thoroughly. CPAs, surgeons, attorneys, psychotherapists, and other specialists may have this power. Connection power comes from organizational and network contacts and supporters. Who some person or group knows is behind this power. Links with wealthy people, ties to politicians, and friendships with CEOs would exemplify this type of power (pp. 252-54; see also, Hoover, 2002, pp. 111-12).

When argumentative resistance factors are estimated, knowledge of the power bases constitutes power. To ignore the power bases is to disadvantage an arguer in advocating a position or dissenting on an issue. If the power base of a person or group in opposition to an idea you are trying to promote is strong, your resistance factor may be high; if the power base is weak, your resistance may be low. Estimating power bases before arguing is wise and may be productive.

Traditionally, argumentation has oftentimes been placed in a context of specialized, and subsequently limited, application. For example, argumentation is explained in formal contexts of debate, discussion, the courts, politics, and so on. For our purposes, argumentation is painted on a wide canvas. It applies not only to special and formal contexts, but to all contexts of human communication, social discourse, public communication, intercultural communication, and human relations. Argumentation involves making points and remaining open to counterpoints; it involves expressing dissenting opinions as well as consenting opinions. Argumentation occurs in diverse contexts, some of which pose tremendous resistance to ideas and evidence and some but minor resistance.

Though argumentation frequently attaches itself to debate and sometimes to discussion, it seems sensible to see argumentation in terms of deliberation. Deliberation, as interpreted here, entails what a legislative body does: debates, discusses, inquiries, questions, converses, clashes, negotiates, bargains, mediates, persuades, influences, and generally makes binding decisions. In relation to ancient arts of discourse, argumentation draws from both rhetoric and dialectic. The rhetorical tradition used in this course respects the persuasive base of Aristotle through the identification ground of Burke. However, it emphasizes an invitational rhetoric of equality, immanent value, and self-determination as explained by Foss and Griffin (1995) with a dialogical ethic of care from Noddings (1984) and a methodology of balance and harmony from Daoist philosophy. The dialectical tradition used here utilizes logic, sophistry, fallacies, and questioning as well as conflict management, interpersonal contradictions, and psychodynamics in human relationships and communication (Baxter & Montgomery, 1996: NY:Guilford, *Relating: Dialogues and Dialectics*; Littlejohn, 2002, pp. 238-43). Subsequently, as we construe the term *argumentation*, dialectics is its foundation and this foundation combines an interest in logical content and humane socio-emotional relations. So, argumentation concerns itself with both content and relational components of controversial communication.

Furthermore, dialectics pertains to ways and means for approaching conflict and harmony as well as division and unity. As Littlejohn puts it, a *"dialectic* is a tension between two or more contradictory elements of a system." Dialectics examines the "ways the system develops or changes, how it moves, in response to [various] tensions." With respect to human communication and relations in controversy, studied dialectically, "relationships are defined and shaped over time by the ways in which partners manage contradictions." In fact, we can assert that the "management of contradiction is the primary force leading to relationship development." In a dialectical exchange, there is a "dynamic interplay of opposing forces" that leads to change. Matters between people are "worked out incrementally and defined as the relationship evolves." Also, dialectics rests on an assumption of totality or wholeness which means that contradictions are inseparable; they "cannot be separated from one another." Each contradiction "entails others, correlates with others, and leads to others" (Littlejohn, 2002, pp. 238-41).

In dialectics, to stress conflict and division, generally speaking, to the exclusion of harmony and unity or to reverse this stress is to create conditions for argumentation that are unmanageable, troublesome, and counterproductive. For example, when arguing, to our detriment, we can follow any of these courses regardless of the consequences: (1) increase conflict without considering harmony; (2) increase harmony without considering conflict; (3) increase division without considering unity; and, (4) increase unity without considering division. We have cautions historically and theoretically with the phenomenon of groupthink and its dire results. If we increase harmony and unity within a group, we can weaken the group, limits its productivity, and create problems within the group, and cause difficulties outside the group (pp.267-69). When we disagree or agree, dissent or consent, we unite with some and divide from others. Our unity with one person or group causes conflict with another; our division from one person or group produces harmony with another. This irony accompanies our dialectical choices when arguing formally or casually. To unite, for instance, with Republicans on one controversial issue may result in our division with Democrats simultaneously on that issue.

The study of argumentation is a study of human communication. Argumentation is a special activity in the broad realm of human communication. Just as communication is not a panacea for the woes of humanity, argumentation is not a panacea for the woes of humanity. In fact, communication and argumentation improperly timed and applied can exacerbate any already troubled human condition. Communication and argumentation are clearly human endeavors that are circumstantially desirable and potentially beneficial. Argumentation can benefit humanity through destructive and constructive means. Hazardous thinking can and should be destroyed while healthy thinking can and should be erected. By analogy, a dilapidated neighborhood should be destroyed so that functional and healthy habitats can be built. For example, in appraising the meaning of a case presented, argumentation assists us in abandoning obsolete evidence to embrace updated evidence.

When we study argumentation, we try to determine what is, and what is not, arguable at any given time. We attempt to work out when we should argue a point and when we should not. To be able to distinguish arguments that are high risk and low risk or foolish and wise is a beneficial end in itself. Studying argumentation should help us determine when and when not to pick a fight or engage in a fight another started. A consciousness of argumentation contributes to our knowledge of argumentative "road signs." That is, borrowing from a common rules of the road manual for comparison, argumentation can, with respect to arguing, teach and guide us on when to proceed with caution, when to stop, when to yield, when to go, when not to enter, when to enter, when not to pass, when to pass, and so on.

Knowing about argumentation fosters an appreciation for what is arguable, controversial enough to argue, and who has the capacity to be argumentative or polemical — that is, who can take part reasonably and productively in controversy and disputation. For example, if we assume a base of 10 in mathematics, is it arguable that $10 + 10$ equals 20? To declare (without stipulating a base of 10) that $10 + 10$ equals 20 is arguable. However, if we assume an American milieu, is the death penalty or legalized prostitution or marijuana decriminalization arguable? A hundred pages from now would not be enough to glut the appetite for argumentation on such topics. Just as we should ask questions about what is arguable, we should also probe into who is conditioned sufficiently to participate productively in sane and rational polemical discourse. We may choose a different time or person with whom to argue on a matter if the person is prone to temper tantrums or violence instead of resolving conflict through reasoned discourse.

When people can and do approach one another for purposes of communication and argumentation, meaning and differences are expressed, are sometimes understood, and are sometimes resolved. When people choose or are ordered to avoid one another and cannot or will not communicate through speech or writing, the opportunity for argumentation to take place in any conventional sense approaches zero. Since communication and meaning occurs in layers, people who fear or hate one another (or are denied contact legally or circumstantially) may be unable or be denied conventional contact or communication. However, communication may occur at other levels symbolically – perhaps as codes of silence and avoidance.

A lack of direct, conventional communication in the form of speech or writing may suggest, at least symbolically, that no conventional communication is desired or permitted. There may be no conversation in any usual sense and certainly no argumentation in the sense of sane, legitimate, rational discourse. Symbolically, the parties may not be willing to talk (or may be prevented from talking) in any ordinary sense. Silence and avoidance prevent direct communication and argumentation from occurring. Argumentation as an ethical discipline and approach to communication goes untapped. In voluntary and ethical contexts, communication and argumentation should not be coerced; both should be practiced freely and without compunction or compulsion. People who are not ready, willing, or able to communicate or argue may not share perspectives; people who are ready, willing, and able to communicate and argue can share perspectives.

From this perspective on argumentation, it is an ethical, communicative act that people perform more or less willingly. This course begins where people are willing and able to engage one another in communication broadly and argumentation specifically. There may be no immediate communicative or argumentative solutions for people unwilling or unable to communicate or argue. If I choose to avoid you and you choose to avoid me, a number of conventional channels of communication are closed. No immediate solution is available to the problems the avoidance creates. If we can and are willing to have contact and clash on differences, courses in communication and argumentation now become potential remedies to relational apprehension and animosity.

The term *argumentation* in this context will be used to embrace human relations and conflict management, the complex communicative acts of arguing and reasoning together, critical thinking and rational assessment of evidence, inquiry into truth and advocacy of a viewpoint, and openness to - and creativity toward - novel ways of dealing with the pursuit of knowledge and the handling of disagreement. Inquiry and advocacy through dialog will interact and alternate: one can inquire into a matter, advocate a position, inquire further, advocate again, and so on continuously improving toward higher orders of decisions and conclusions. Argumentation thus includes the tradition of reasoning as derived from rhetoric, dialectic, and logic as well as the tradition of dialogue as derived from psychology, communication, and forensics. Argumentation includes discourse in the form of a political or legal monologue, but it also draws from everyday conversations and discussions. In short, argumentation studies formal exchanges of conflict. Argumentation also studies the ethnomethodology

(Garfinkel, 1967) of argumentation – that is, how people disagree with others and assert themselves in daily life.

In the broad sense of *argumentation* offered above, competency is the objective and expectation in this text, not mastery. Your desired objective with respect to argumentation as a blend of content and relationship might be reasonably stated as high competency. As a result of this or any single course in argumentation, to expect mastery on both the content and relational components of argumentation may be admirably ambitious but unrealistic. Mastery on both is rare. Who has attained mastery on both would be debatable: Socrates, Lao-tsu, Sir Thomas More, Sri Arubindo, Simone de Beauvoir, L. Susan Stebbing, Suzanne Langer, Johnny Cochrane? While many who practice argumentation achieve competence, even high competence, who has attained mastery on this challenging communicative enterprise is debatable. To be optimistic, it will be assumed that there are masters of argumentation in the sense defined, and those mentioned may be candidates as masters of argumentation, but no pronouncement will be made now. If you feel comfortable later and are willing to support your assertion, you are invited to declare who you believe are masters of argumentation.

Many texts explain argumentation in relation to courtroom debate, public debate, parliamentary deliberation, or public discussion. A prevailing theme in argumentation involves how to win and beat an opponent. The language of the texts approaches at times the strategies described in manuals and accounts of prizefighting and military combat. The game strategy is usually one of winning over an opponent who loses. While ethical premises for the verbal fray are established, the justifiable goal is one of overcoming an opponent. Although this strategy and language dominate debate texts, discussion texts can also be combative. Occasionally, a debate text addresses a less combative form of conflict oftentimes referred to as problem-solving debate. In problem-solving debate, concessions can be made for the benefit of the group at large. Of course, in the argumentation of group discussion, the benefit of the group is a preeminent concern.

Let me make this perfectly clear. Looking at argumentation on a win-lose basis is traditionally and ethically acceptable and justifiable; it may very well constitute the norm. Many professions require and demand a winning knowledge and ability in a win-lose situation. Most argumentation texts address this interest: how to win over opposition in debates, discussion, and even conversations. Someone wins; someone loses. You are cast in the role of the combatant coached to win. The authors advance strategies to attain a win and avoid a loss. American society, as we know it in law and politics and commerce at least, may not exist without this give and take form of communication and without winning as a goal. Argumentation, as we see it, thus encompasses: (1) the traditional persuasion of

29

Aristotle with the theme that rhetoric requires a sound dialectic: that is, ethical persuasion rests on logos (reason) with added power from ethos (character) and pathos (emotion); and (2) the contemporary notion from Foss and Griffin of an invitational rhetoric: a proposed theory of ethical persuasion that is more a dialogue than a monologue, and draws from feminist sources, and compatible with Asiatic ethics.

The materials you may read in studying argumentation for our purposes cover the win-lose strategies and tactics of argumentation; these materials can be applied to argumentative situations with severity or with leniency. The goal remains, however, to beat an opponent. There is a place in this course for traditional, hard forms of argumentation. The hard forms of argumentation require, though, a different set of skills, attitudes, and knowledge to apply successfully. Hard forms of arguing may occur in courts, public debates, police interrogations, and journalistic interviews; they may also occur in family and personal disagreements. Although in this course you may chose to develop the hard forms of argumentation, I ask you to try a genteel form of argumentation. The genteel form with its demand for alternate skill, attitudes, and knowledge is clarified next and detailed later. Whether you chose a hard form of argumentation or the mindful dialectic soon to be detailed, any rational attack on an argument would be wise to follow the critical plan Infante provides along with any other critical means this text provides.

The form of argumentation promoted in this context is for an arguer's classroom and lifelong benefit and entails what I call a "mindful dialectic." The term *dialectic* is used here as a rough equivalent to the term *argumentation* and is used oftentimes to refer to any form of interpersonal clash or conflict (especially verbal) and its escalation or resolution. Broadly speaking, *dialectics* deals with the study and treatment of opposition, contradiction, and discrepancy. Although it has a long and rich academic history, the word *dialectic* has less currency in modern day English than the word *argumentation.* In ordinary English, several terms have negative charges despite the efforts of the academic world to make the term *argumentation* and its derivatives positive and beneficial. Although being *argumentative* is an example of a negative use in ordinary language and legal circles, it is used favorably in the field of communication. The contrary tones for the term *argumentative* do not make a student's life easy, nor does it make a student's study of argumentation immediately sensible. In an effort to respect academic tradition and the current meanings associated with terms, I will be using the term *dialectic* interchangeably with *argumentation* while at the same time using the term *argumentation* and its derivatives (e.g., *argue, arguer,* and *argument)* favorably. However, I will also use terms that are favorable alternatives for *argumentation* and its derivatives (e.g., *advocate, inquirer,* and *questioner*).

To minimize our vulnerability to fallacious thinking and to inhibited communication between parties on issues, sensitive and polite yet rigorous argumentation (that is, the mindful dialectic) is proposed as a worthwhile alternative to traditional modes of argumentation as well as to mindless modes of argumentation. The mindful dialectic mode of argumentation covers reasoning together with sensitivity to and respect for the feelings and capacities of all parties involved. Interpersonal sensitivity guides the dialectic in order to gain heightened mutual interpersonal understanding and shared adherence to at least relative truth. My explanation of this method will be presented soon and is consistent with theory formulated by diverse argumentation theorists.

SELECTED VIEWS OF ARGUMENTATION

Argumentation is a complex topic with numerous theorizers. Some modern theorizers include: Stephen Toulmin, Frans van Eemeren, Chaim Perelman, Wayne Brockriede, Barbara Warnick, Charles Williard, Sonja Foss and Karen Foss, Josina Makau and Debian Marty, Richard Rieke and Malcom Sillars, Andrea Lunsford, J. Vernon Jensen, Dominic Infante, Austin Freeley, this author, and others. Additional writers on argumentation will be used to review the notion of argumentation. This perspective on argumentation draws its conception of argumentation from the following writers on this topic, and the notion of argumentation advanced here coincides especially with the ideas about argumentation these authors advance: Makau and Marty, Infante, Eemeren and Grootendorst, and Foss and Foss. This perspective also draws from traditions of thought that have reflected on and utilized conflict, even if the theorizing is only indirectly dialectical or rhetorical: for example, perspectives on the existential dialog, zen perceptions, and psychotherapeutic practices (especially Rational-emotive, Rogerian, and Gestalt).

The most panoramic view of argumentation may be presented by Lundsford, Ruszkiewicz, and Walters (2004). Each text (for example, written, spoken, visual) is a "potential argument" (p. v). Any text that "expresses a point of view" can be an argument. Every text is an argument "designed to influence" readers, listeners, viewers, and respondents in general (p. 4). Yet, argument is not merely about winning. Although many arguments target winning and language has an "argumentative edge that aims to make a point, not all language use aims to win out over others." Some argumentation is invitational (derived from Foss and Griffin, 1995) and tries not to conquer others but to create or

31

discover a ground for mutual regard and exploration. In addition to winning, persuading, and changing others points of view, argumentation is used "to inform, to explore, to make decisions, even to meditate or pray" (p. 6).

Furthermore, argumentation may be based on "finding common ground and establishing trust among those who disagree about issues, and on approaching audiences in nonthreatening ways." Those who follow Rogerian (derived from the psychotherapist Carl Rogers) methods of argumentation strive to "understand the perspectives of those with whom they disagree, looking for 'both/and' or 'win/win' solutions (rather than 'either/or' or 'win/lose' ones) whenever possible." An unmeasured amount of successful argumentation today seems to follow "such principles, consciously or not" (p. 7). By treating every text as a potential argument, the authors encourage everyone to proceed in the "never-ending conversation about our lives and the world," a conversation sometimes called "academic inquiry," with the rigorous standard of taking "no claim at face value," examining "all evidence thoroughly," and studying the implications of our beliefs and the beliefs of others. An inquiring approach to argumentation might thus produce a healthy suspicion about the arguments presented to us daily (p. 24).

Richard Rieke and Malcom Sillars (1975) define *argumentation* as an "ongoing transaction of advancing claims, supporting them with reasons, and the advancing of competing claims with appropriate support, the mutual criticism of them, and the granting of adherence to one" (p. 7). J. Vernon Jensen (1981) places argumentation in the "overall framework of the human communication process." He adds that negative meanings associated with argumentation should be dispelled. In our daily language, we speak of argumentative people as those who are "troublesome, unfriendly, quarrelsome." In contrast, Jensen sees argumentative people as those engaged in "presenting and examining claims and reasons." Those who argue reasonably have a counterpoint in those who do not: that is, those who participate in a "communicative exchange in which countering claims are exchanged with virtually no supporting reasons and with virtually no examination of each other's claims" (p. 5).

Dominic Infante makes a distinction between aggressive communication (especially verbal aggression) which is destructive and argumentation which is constructive. He explains that the term *argumentativeness* is the "ability to recognize controversial issues in communication situations, to present and defend positions on the issues, and to attack the positions which other people take." Infante adds that there are degrees of argumentative ability. He refers to these abilities as *argumentative competence.* Argumentative competence, according to Infante, involves these actions: (1) stating the controversy in the form of a proposition, (2) analyzing propositions and inventing arguments to support a position and attack another position, (3) presenting and defending one position, (4) attacking another position, and (5) managing interpersonal relations during a conflict. Because a conflict involves potentially conflict and disagreement, two socially difficult barriers of communication to surmount, managing interpersonal conflict is important in any discussion of argumentation and is crucial to the courteously rigorous argumentation method advanced in this course (Infante, 1988). [Note: Later, you will be assigned to read pages 45-54 and 69-80 from Infante for the argumentation assignments presented above. You may read them now if you like, but you will not be tested on these until Lesson 3.}

Inch and Warnick (2002, p.4) define *argumentation* as the "process of making arguments intended to justify beliefs, attitudes, and values so as to influence others." These theorists distinguish it from critical thinking in this way. Critical thinking "does not necessarily involve communication," but "argumentation does." They also stress the context of controversial discourse and of controversy itself. In their account of the term *argument*, Inch and Warnick define it as a "set of statements in which a claim is made, support is offered for it, and there is an attempt to influence someone in a context of disagreement" (p. 6). Of course, they distinguish an argument in this sense from "interpersonal arguments or disputes" (Ibid).

Eisenberg and Ilardo (1972) describe *argumentation* broadly as referring to the "field of inquiry made up of the basic principles of logic and rhetoric that underlie reasoned discourse." Moreover, argumentation, as they see it, "does not ignore those ways of influencing others that fall outside the category of 'reasoned discourse' – such as personal influence or emotional appeals." However, argumentation emphasizes the "*logical* aspects of argument" through its primary concern with the "logical proof of propositions." Discourse that lacks solid reasoning and proof may be studied in argumentation so that the rational elements that are missing may become manifest. Distinguishing between persuasion and argumentation, Eisenberg and Ilardo tell us that persuasion aims to change minds "by virtually any means short of physical force while argumentation aims to establish "conclusions through reasoned discourse." Subsequently, most propaganda would constitute persuasion, not argumentation. Argumentation as a critical method may be used with benefit to show deficiencies and excesses that are usually present in the efforts of propaganda (pp. 2-3).

To Austin Freeley (1986), *argumentation* means giving reasons in "communicative situations by people whose purpose is the justification of acts, beliefs, attitudes, and values." He mentions several common and worthwhile applications of argumentation. One is the arena of individual decisions, discussion, and debate. When we can make a decision without approval from others, we can make informed individual decisions after considering the arguments for or against a plan of action or pattern of thought. When we need the "consent or cooperation of others to carry out our decision," we seek rational ways to secure their support through debate, discussion, or a combination of these methods. Again, persuasion, propaganda, coercion, and other extra-rational forms of influence can be analyzed through argumentation yet fall outside its circumference. In this course, the rational elements of discussion and debate, dialog broadly speaking, constitute the focus of argumentation (pp. 2-8).

Another valuable perspective on argumentation is offered by Makau and Marty (2001). To these theorists, *argumentation* is a "communication process people use to understand and make sense of differing perspectives on a given topic, and to help them decide where they stand on relevant issues" (p. 81). They distinguish several negative uses of the term *argumentation*. To some it means "engaging in a hostile shouting match"; for some it connotes "irrational, emotionally volatile conflict between individuals"; for some it is to win arguments through "aggressive confrontation"; and, for some it is a "form of combative interaction" (Ibid). Instead, Makau and Marty approach argumentation and disagreement as a "process of reasoned interaction intended to help participants and audiences make the best assessments or the best decisions in any given situation" (p. 87).

Makau and Monty (2001) envision argumentation as being cooperative in the creation of a deliberative community and see "those who disagree with us as resources rather than as rivals" (p. 88), a view similar to that explained above of Foss and Foss on invitational rhetoric and similar to the explanation of the mindful dialectic soon to follow. In short, instead of viewing those who differ from us as adversaries, they are viewed as partners. Those participating in cooperative argumentation know that their viewpoints can "only be enlightened by as comprehensive and open an exchange as possible" (p. 87). Makau and Marty urge us to confront disagreement ethically and effectively. They maintain that "efforts to suppress or otherwise avoid addressing disagreements almost inevitably lead to even greater conflict." Rather than avoiding conflict and disagreement, we must "develop tools for confronting disagreement peacefully, ethically, and effectively" (p. 8). Furthermore, to be successful in demonstrating that we take alternative perspectives seriously, we are advised to work from these premises: (1) "every perspective is necessarily partial"; (2) "alternative viewpoints enhance our own understanding precisely because they represent other sides of a 'story'"; and, (3) our perspectives on complex issues develop interdependently because of "our fundamental interdependence" (p. 11). In short, these theorists respect disagreement as "a key element of communal deliberations" that can become fair and well-informed decisions that are understandable (p. 7).

The Dutch school of argumentation defines *argumentation* as a "speech act consisting of a constellation of statements designed to justify or refute an expressed opinion and calculated in a regimented discussion to convince a rational judge of a particular standpoint in respect of the acceptability or unacceptability of that expressed opinion." The primary scholars of the Dutch school are Frans van Eemeren and Rob Grootendorst (1983). Their notion of argumentation includes the concept and term of *dialectic*. Eemeren and Grootendorst of the University of Amsterdam endorse a dialectical approach to argumentation that aims to "establish how debates must be conducted for the critical testing of expressed opinions." Argumentation thus becomes a "part of a critical discussion about an expressed opinion," and a critical discussion entails an interaction between "a protagonist and an antagonist of a particular standpoint in respect of an expressed opinion." The purpose of the discussion is to determine whether the "protagonist's standpoint is defensible against the critical reactions of the antagonist." In a dialog or discussion that is critical, it must in principle be possible for "pro-argumentation and contra-argumentation to be put forward." The arguers are supposed to adopt the position of rational judges who react critically to the argumentative communication to ensure critical discourse ensues (Van Eemeren & Grootendorst, pp. 177-178). Once again, in this course, the terms *dialectic* and *argumentation* are used interchangeably: *dialectic* being the name for the broadest notion of arguing in the form of a dialogue or discussion but also in the form of a monologue or debate.

The Mindful Dialectic Perspective

Few students today are not familiar with the *Star War* series. Please indulge me on this comparison to "The Force" in the *Star War* series. Argumentation as a discipline may draw from the "light" and the "dark" sides of "The Force." While the light and the dark sides are simplifications for our purposes, this metaphor will be used metaphorically to call attention to the fact that argumentation applies to mindful and mindless, soft and hard, kind and cruel, or gentle and hurtful (that is, light or dark) forms and methods in everyday life. In argumentation, broadly speaking, light and dark or gentle and hurtful sources and methods are used daily. Unlike the simplifications of the light and dark sides of The Force, argumentation must sometimes draw from both sides to establish truth, dispute falsehood, uncover deceit, reveal a lie, and so on. In commercial, scientific, and legal arenas, hard and soft forms of argumentation are tapped for the benefit of all involved. At its best, argumentation can be reasonable, practical, and intelligent. Of course, according to Toulmin, since rational procedures embody themselves in actual communicators who are reasoning, rational procedures are "things which are learned, employed, sometimes modified, on occasion even abandoned, by the people doing the reasoning." In the mindful dialectic, depending on circumstances and intentions, argumentation can fluctuate from reasonableness to the abandonment of reasonableness to accomplish an end if the situation so demands. The mindful dialectic recognizes that oppressors with unjust power in oppressive situations may need to be addressed in a radically different form of argumentation than reasonable people in accountable and democratic contexts. Hence, the practical argumentation of the mindful dialectic must be, as Foss, Foss, and Trapp explain Toulmin (2002, pp. 125 & 127), "emancipated from the hegemony of theoretical argument." Reasonability rules over the tyranny of analytical theory. Through the mindful dialectic, arguing in a loud whisper is preferred exponentially to arguing in a loud shout. However, the mindful dialectic includes the loud shout when the ethics of the circumstances require it.

In the context of the mindful dialectic, argumentation becomes the setting forth of a thesis with evidence in contexts that embody degrees of human acceptance, manipulation, deception, malice, confusion, resistance, and opposition. Argumentation deals with probabilities and audiences and becomes dialectics. Dialectics is seen as the study and practice of proactively balancing harmony and disharmony among communicators; it is the proactive pursuit of disagreement in agreement and agreement in disagreement. Dialecticians are viewed here as those communicators who seek the truth and who try to establish what is and is not a common ground between communicators; they incite dissent as the healthy counterpart of consent and disagreement as the healthy counterpart of agreement. Their interest is primarily in the audience and relational concerns; but they have competitive secondary interests in the reasons, content, facts, and reasoning. Pictorially, this complementary relationship can be seen as a yin-yang symbol with agreement or consent in one part and disagreement or dissent in the other part. To remain consistent with Lao-tsu's leaning on the Dao, the symbol favors somewhat the yin of agreement and consent over the yang of disagreement and dissent:

Complements in a Dialectical System of Communication

{Agreement/Disagreement}
{Consonance/Dissonance}
{Stimulus/Response}
{Point/Counterpoint}

36

{Question/Response}

{Social Influence/Resistance}

{Advocacy/Opposition}

{Order/Disobedience}

{Acceptance/Rejection}

{Compliance/Non-Compliance}

{Tension/Resolution}

{Invitation/Enfoldment}

{Attack/Counterattack}

{Attack/Block}

{Attack/Evasion}

{Attack/Redirect}

{Attack/Absorb}

{Progress/Regress}

{Pro/Con}

{Positive/Negative}

{Competition/Cooperation}

{Approach/Avoid}

{For/Against}

{Fight/Flee}

{Fight/Freeze)

{Hard/Soft}

{Yin/Yang}

{Thesis/Antithesis}

The value of the daily use of argumentation is debatable; it can be hurtful rather than helpful, can provide far more heat than light, wound rather than heal, and can be mindless rather than mindful. Mindful is contrasted here with mindless (Langer, 1989; Burgoon, Berger, & Waldron, 2000) as states of relative awareness ranging from extremely high to zero (DeVito, 2003). In its lofty places, mindfulness would constitute a widely knowledgeable person or a so-called enlightened person. In its lowly places, mindlessness would constitute an extremely ignorant person or totally uninspired person.

Most of us are mindful on some topics and mindless on others. Being mindful on topics relevant to our interests is our noble goal in the present context.

In the mindful dialectic proposed, the accent will be on the light side of The Force: the forms and sources of argumentation that are soft, kind, and gentle yet progressive. The mindful dialectic requires its arguers to be good-natured and encourages them to be good-humored – if possible, to inject humor and levity into the dispute as often as conditions permit. The mindful dialectic can be open-ended as in public discussion or close-ended as in public debate. To be mindful when you argue means in this course to be all those virtues that sensitivity training strives to attain: namely, caring, delicate, careful, prudent, cautious, nurturing, considerate, compassionate, sympathetic, empathic, daring, strong, reasonable, knowledgeable, and – when possible - humorous. To strive for and implement these virtues is to be mindful. Dialectic in this course means, once again, the acts of verbal and nonverbal communication clashes, conflicts, disagreements, contradictions and their escalation or diffusion.

You will find that much of the mindful dialectic is rooted broadly in the ethical virtues of caring, wisdom, and compassion – even love and forgiveness. Caring, wisdom, and compassion as ethical grounds will be discussed later in the course. For now, you might note that caring, wisdom, and compassion have ancient and modern sources. Some of the cultural sources include: the humane and feminist writings of Nel Noddings (1984) on the feminine ethic of care, the feminist perspective from Sonja K. Foss and Cindy L. Griffin (1995 & 2002) of an invitational rhetoric, Rosenberg's (2005) language of non-violent communication, Wayne Brockriede's notion of arguers as lovers, Martin Buber's dialogic ethic, the Buddhist ethic of compassion, the Jain ethic of *ahimsa* (or being neither violent nor hurtful), and the Judeo-Christian value (as institutionalized in the USA and Canada) of showing sympathetic and compassionate concern for others. Of course, other ethical, moral, hygienic, and therapeutic systems that treat others with sane and reasonable care have contributed to the mindful dialectic as well.

The challenge with the mindful dialectic perspective is to pursue understanding, meaning, and knowledge of a person or issue in everyday interpersonal life through gentle yet rigorous means. The goal is to pursue a controversial matter without triggering inhibition, concealment, defensiveness, avoidance, hostility, embarrassment, repression, and other human reactions that prevent an arguer seeking information through dialog from unfolding and reaching a worthwhile goal. While harsh methods may work in various daily arenas, I am not asking you to use such methods in this class. It will be enough to proceed with the long-range benefits the sensitive dialectic perspective permits.

While a hurtful method may be temporarily needed to benefit the arguer circumstantially for short-range ethical purposes, the method of arguing provided by the mindful dialectic that encourages all to proceed toward knowledge in a nonthreatening and supportive environment should remain the long-range and overall norm.

While recognizing unfavorable conditions for argumentation, the mindful dialectic perspective on argumentation involves the creation of favorable conditions to make it a success. The favorable conditions (or virtues) a mindful dialectic aims to embody and maximize include these: sensitivity, care, delicacy, carefulness, consideration, compassion, sympathy, empathy, sincerity, unconditional positive regard, openness, responsibility, honesty, involvement, authenticity, transparency, legitimacy, forgiveness, and love. The mindful dialectic tries to be inquisitive, curious, critical, and even contentious as decently, consciously, conscientiously, sensitively, courteously, and politely as possible under the circumstances with a particular person or group. The strategy here is to be critical yet creative, issue-centered yet personality-conscious, logical yet humane, and willing to disagree (or agree) and probe as imaginatively and kindly as possible.

This dialectical perspective will also try to minimize unfavorable conditions (or vices): specifically, the opposites of the virtues listed above. The mindful dialectic aims to avoid, reduce, or eliminate especially these vices: being abusive insulting, quarrelsome, threatening, mindless, aggressive, inhumane, deceitful, aloof, manipulative, exploitative, careless, and malicious. The sensitive dialectic applauds whatever enhances disclosure; it decries whatever inhibits disclosure. The goal of the sensitive dialectic is to contest matters intellectually only; there is no interest in attacking a person or undermining a personality. Punitive consequences to asking and answering questions or asserting a proposition and responding to it have limited space in this dialectic.

A dialog employing the perspective of the mindful dialectic attempts to purify as much as possible harsh, mindless, and hard methods of argumentation; it substitutes as much as possible methods of argumentation that are humane, mindful, and therapeutic. The light part of the mindful dialectic must override its dark side considerably like daytime in the summer around the 60th parallel with its approximately 20 hours of light hours and four of dark hours. To advance in any other manner risks the pitfalls in a voluntary exchange of differences mentioned above; the parties to the dialog concerning conflicts, questions, or contradictions may suffer various inhibitions, avoidance, hostility, and the like. Consequently, an insensitive approach to acquiring information interpersonally may have to be abandoned. The mindful dialectic asks many questions. The following three overlapping questions summarize the interests of the mindful dialectic with relative accuracy: (1) Will the argumentation be worth the risk? (2) Can the argumentation be acquired without punitive consequences to the parties involved? And, 3) Will the benefit outweigh the cost enough to justify the risk of argumentation? The overriding mindfully dialectical questions might be: Can the circumstances be arranged is such a way that arguing in a loud whisper will get an ethically desired result, or is it necessary to step outside the norm of arguing in a loud whisper to accomplish an ethically desired end?

Argumentation as a mindful dialectic recognizes the light and dark or hard and soft methods available to discussants, debaters, or, broadly, communicators. The mindful dialectic sides with the powers related to light. By analogy, it targets a day with 20 light hours and four dark hours, not vice-versa. To make headway with the mindful dialectic approach to argumentation, no one needs a day with 24 light hours. However, a day with no light hours or but several will not support the objective of an open dialog. Yet, the mindful dialectic is pushy in a gentle way like yoga. The attempt is not to violate the other. A Western version of *ahimsa* or non-violence pervades the effort. When possible, like a yogi stretching nonviolently to a maximum, in the mindful dialectic, the arguer stretches one another's views as far as each will go without violating the arguers or methods involved. Occasionally and circumstantially, an ungentle and coarse method of argumentation my have to supplant the norm of non-violence. Caring ethics may demand that when others may be hurt by the consequences of a norm of arguing honestly in a loud whisper, the arguers may have to shout, scream, or remain silent in order to help someone at risk.

The communicators remain considerate of one another at all times and mindless as seldom as possible. Between meaning emerging from the content being discussed and meaning emerging from the relationship with the other, the meaning from the content must be held as having a weight never to exceed 49 percent while the meaning from the relationships with the other must have a weight never to fall short of 51 percent. This ratio of 49 to 51 as maximum and minimum standards resembles the tendency of the communication pattern present in high-context Asian cultures, such as, Japan and Thailand. The relationship must be held to be of greater value for a robust dialog to continue indefinitely than the content desired. If sensitivities require, the pursuit of content must be delayed until a time when trust and confidence allows the acquisition of knowledge to advance. A discussion or debate must remain open to eliciting disclosure and to expressing conflict. To argue whisperingly constitutes the end in view.

Hard forms of argumentation certainly will yield for some the exuberance of the thrill of victory. To avoid the agony of defeat, arguers who get rough with one another may indulge in harsh forms of argumentation: forms definitely suited for special competitive circumstances (perhaps, courts, political debates, and so on). The psychology and methods surrounding hard forms of argumentation are difficult in a manner radically different from the psychology and methods surrounding the mindful dialectic. One can be skilled potentially in both forms but is likely to have one form dominate. A prosecuting attorney may favor the hard form while a psychotherapist may favor the mindful dialectic. Since circumstances and people are never the same, arguers must vary and differ in their mode of arguing.

Those practicing the hard, and sometimes mindless, forms of argumentation may be satisfied with a short-range victory while those practicing the mindful dialectic will only be satisfied with long-term victory. Those choosing the mindful dialectic see the short-range accomplishments resulting from hard forms of argumentation as Pyrrhic victories – immediate benefits coupled with eventual setbacks and disasters. Planning for long-range victories has its singular challenges over planning for immediate victories. Indeed, depending on circumstances, those engaging in the mindful dialectic would likely view hard forms of argumentation, generally, as forms of conditionally mindless Pyrrhic arguing: for example, winning the debate but losing the sale, winning the argument but losing a spouse, and so on. Winning over time replaces winning now as a goal for those using the method of the mindful dialectic; distant and overall benefits without drawbacks and backlashes take precedence over immediate and limited benefits with drawbacks and backlashes.

The quest of the mindful dialectic is not to dominate (or to dominate incidentally at most) another in a conversation, dialog, discussion, or debate; rather, the quest is to, with kind and non-violent communication manners and at a pace suitable to all parties to the interaction, discover meaning and identify knowledge of actions, attitudes, facts, goodness, truth, beauty, justice, and so on. In a general way, two ends exist: one objective is to employ a communication method that allows the arguers to understand one another and share information among themselves while the other objective is to reduce or eliminate misunderstand and misinformation among the arguers. These objectives must be sought with rigorous yet creative intelligence by arguing in loud whispers.

In pursuing the mindful dialectic, we do not have to presume that other arguers are as fragile as empty eggshells to pressure, challenge, and conflict. Indeed, by debating and discussing matters with others sensitively, interpersonal trust and strength increases. Instead of feeling obliged to approach others with "kid gloves" or as if they were delicate figurines, with the building of interpersonal respect, the clash can become more outspoken than clashes that occur under hostile or aggressive circumstances. When we respect a person's limits in the mindful dialectic, we also respect that person's powers. If the opponent is strong enough to handle heavy criticism, then we may deliver heavy criticism while honoring that person's potential limits. We give one another as much as each can take. Our pursuit is good-natured and good-humored. If we must pull a punch, we do so. If the person can take a solid punch, we deliver one. If we can tease or joke about an issue without reducing the dignity of the other, we may do so. We judge mindfully one another's strengths and weakness. Instead of capitalizing on one another's weaknesses, we cater to one another's strengths. In the language of the philosopher Martin Buber, we develop an I-Thou relationship far more than an I-It relationship.

In this orientation, we are free to use the hard, although ethical, methods of argumentation elaborated in the readings or the sensitive dialectic I suggest. In short, go for it! In fact, I challenge you to go for it and be other than gentle and genteel when a gentle and genteel approach to argumentation would suffice. When you write your argumentative responses to the exercises, you can use whatever form you like without reprisal. Prove the powers or weaknesses of the mindful dialectic by experimentation. You are free to blend or combine hard and soft forms of argumentation. The choice is yours. Your only obligation is that you must give your best argument or counter-argument to any case presented. Assume your instructor is tough enough to be open to your viewpoint as supported by your reasoning and evidence. I urge you to be sensitive, nonetheless, and proceed with the efficacy and wisdom of diplomacy. However, you should not argue mindlessly. Mindlessness in this approach to argumentation should be seen as a vice. Now get busy in the building of mindful cases.

Since they describe what I am talking about in an alternative manner, material from Eisenberg and Ilardo (1972) will be discussed at this time. They distinguish on an argumentative continuum among a fight, altercation, debate, discussion, and dialogue with a fight at one extreme and a dialog at the other. Their explanation of "dialogue" corresponds closely to the mindful dialectic explained here; their "fight" corresponds closely to hard argumentation – a ruffian's approach to controversy. Viewing an argument as "any kind of disagreement between two or more persons" (p. 3), Eisenberg and Ilardo portray a fight as being high and a dialogue low in negative and hostile emotionality, a fight offering maximum resistance to new ideas and a dialogue as providing open-mindedness to new ideas, a fight using the lowest level and a dialogue the highest level of language, and a fight requires the least and a dialogue the most years of formal education and knowledge of the subject of disagreement. When it comes to written rules, a fight and a dialogue have the least while debate has the most. However, when it comes to unwritten rules, a fight and a dialogue have the most while a debate the least (pp. 4-13). Emotional components are crucial to the consideration of whether to pursue a disagreement and how to purse it if one must.

The psychologist C. G. Jung (The undiscovered self, Boston: Little Brown, 1958) held that "rational argument can be conducted with some prospect of success only so long as the emotionality of a given situation does not exceed a certain critical degree." If the temperature of arguers rises above a certain level, the "possibility of reason's having any effect ceases and its place it taken by slogans and chimerical wish-fantasies" (p. 5). Subsequently, according to Eisenberg and Ilardo, a fight will likely yield strong negative and hostile emotions in contrast to a dialogue (p. 4). A dialogue may yield strong and favorable feelings, not powerful anger.

Illustrations of the Mindful Dialectic

Numerous illustrations of the mindful dialectic can be found in historical as well as contemporary sources, real as well as fictional sources. The dialogs of Socrates provide excellent examples of a balance between rigorous reasoning on the one hand and psychological sensitivity on the other. The apostolic accounts of Jesus Christ's conversations with authorities and citizens, the *Analects* of Confucius, and interactions with the Dalai Lama (Hopkins, 1992) provide rich examples. The psychotherapeutic interviews of Fritz Perls, Carl Rogers, and Albert Ellis provide fine examples. Most of the interviews of Barbara Walters as a broadcast journalist (especially her interviews of Ronald Reagan and Clint Eastwood) and almost all the interviews of Oprah Winfrey would demonstrate the mindful dialectic elegantly. Many, but not all, of the dialogs between Larry King, Charlie Rose, and William F. Buckley, Jr. and their interviewees give us superb illustrations of the mindful dialectic as well.

Fictional scripts supply numerous instances of the mindful dialectic. In the *Star War* series, the dialog between Obi-wan Kenobi and Luke Skywalker as well as those between Yoda and Luke Skywalker are paramount examples. In Carlos Castaneda's series of stories on the medicine man Don Juan, he has volumes of dialogs that illustrate the mindful dialectic. For an especially clear example, in DeVito's *Messages* (1996) text on pages 80-81, two scripts are borrowed from psychotherapists Carl Rogers and Richard Farson. The script from Example 1 would illustrate a hard form of argumentation while the script from Example 2 would illustrate the mindful dialectic. All of these sources just cited will give you lucid examples of the mindful dialectic.

REFLECTIONS: Agreements, Conflicts, and Questions

　　To demonstrate the continually and reasonably critical aspect of argumentative discourse, after each unit, reflections will be offered. The reflections attempt to force you to evaluate and reexamine whatever is asserted, explained, or claimed in the units by any of the contributors. As for perspectives on argumentation, is not too much made of the nature of argumentation? Are the definitions too broad or too vague? Why should a communicator be considerate of someone who is an advocate of another view or cause? Is there any ground to think of argumentation as anything but a fight? Dialectics is just a fancy word for quarrelling, is it not? Argumentation is simply about fighting and winning by any means necessary, correct? Why should someone be concerned about long-range argumentation? All argumentation is like a battle that you win or lose now, is that not so? Why is so much made about a mindful dialectic that is sensitive on many levels? A mindful dialectic is just a gutless excuse for avoiding a fight? Arguing is hard and should not be seen as having any soft parts, true?

LESSON TWO

Language in Argumentation

Lesson Objectives:

To explain the formulations of questions and propositions in argumentation

To provide an overview of the role of language in argumentation

To discuss sexist language concerns

To present contributions to argumentation from language studies

OUTLINE FOR KEY TERMS FOR THIS UNIT

1. Propositions and/or Questions: Fact, Value, and Policy

2. Probes: Questions and/or Imperatives - Open, Closed, Direct, Leading

Questions and Propositions in Debate and Discussion

Commonly, the following three classifications of propositions or questions are typically found in texts on argumentation. Whether the text relates argumentation to the public or closed arenas of debate or of discussion, these three statements occur. Statements in the form of declarative sentences are called *propositions* and those in the form of interrogative sentences are called *questions.* Debate and discussion propositions and questions emerge from and express a focus for differences in a controversy.

People differ and can express how they differ through propositions and questions of fact, value, and policy in statements suited for debate or discussion. Debate statements tend to create a divisive climate for communication and argumentation while the discussion statements tend to create an inclusive climate (Eisenberg & Ilardo, 1972, pp. 26-27; Infante, 1988, pp. 34-36; Hoover, 2002, pp. 84-86).

The structural and grammatical distinction between debate and discussion statements is crucial to predicting communication outcomes. To illustrate the distinction between statements of fact, value, and policy suited to debate and to discussion, an elaboration follows. Using a policy statement to help explain differences, debate statements create a close-ended response: "The USA should deport illegal aliens" or "Should the USA deport illegal aliens?" Stated in this manner, communicators argue that the USA should or should not in response to the question that creates a communicative situation in which respondents support or oppose the question. Using a policy statement to help explain differences, discussion statements create an open-ended response: "The USA should do something about its illegal aliens" or "What should the USA do about its illegal aliens?"

Stated in this manner, communicators discuss what policy the USA should institute on illegal aliens. Several plans may surface and be discussed. All may be rejected, two may be combined, new plans may emerge, and so on. Stated for debate or for discussion, both forms have their useful place. However, you should be conscious of the two differing formulations and use each for the end you wish to attain. You do not want to formulate a debate question when you desire open-ended responses; you do not want to formulate a discussion question when you desire close-ended responses.

Probes: Open, Closed, Direct, and Leading

In communication in general and argumentation in particular, *probes* take the form of questions and imperatives. Probes are linguistic and rhetorical devices used to acquire information from respondents. Questions and imperatives should be used ethically and strategically in argumentation. Questions would be interrogative sentences and imperatives would be imperative sentences – sentences uttering a command, order, request, or polite request. The content in either form would be equivalent. Although the preference in argumentation and communication texts generally is to discuss questions explicitly, imperatives are at least implied. We will stress questions, cover imperatives, yet be explicit about both.

Of the diverse classification of types of question and imperative probes, the chosen three here are those of open, closed, direct, and leading questions and imperatives. Open questions and imperatives open the respondent to an unrestricted and unlimited response. The person's response may be a mere shoulder shrug or a lengthy reply of an hour or more. In principle, the end of the questioner and requester is to allow the respondent to be open and disclose much. For example, "Why did you shift from the Democratic to the Republican Party?" The command version of this open question is its imperative form: "Tell me (or Please tell me) why you shifted from the Democratic to the Republican Party." Closed question and imperatives restrain the respondent to a restricted and limited response. The person's response may any of these brief replies: yes, no, true, false, undecided, I don't know, and so on ad infinitum. In principle, the end of the questioner and requester is to allow the respondent to answer in as brief a way as conceivable and to volunteer nothing else. For example, "Are you now a

Democrat?" The command version of this question is its imperative form: "Tell me (or Please tell me) whether you are now a Democrat?"

Direct and leading questions and imperatives will be explained together. Leading questions and imperatives occur in a context in which someone does not know you have an answer but assumes you have one. The questioner and requester expect you to reply and reveal something about a matter that has not been established. Otherwise, the questions and imperatives are direct. When a fact is known to a questioner and to the respondent, the question probe is simply direct. An established example of a leading form of probe is: "When were you last arrested for smoking marijuana?" The imperative form of this leading question is: "Tell me (or Please tell me) when you were last arrested for smoking marijuana?" Assuming you never smoked marijuana, were never arrested for smoking marijuana, and never smoked marijuana in a region where it was illegal, the questioner has established none of these through the question: (a) that you have smoked marijuana on at least one occasion; (b) that you have smoked marijuana and arrested for it at least once; and (c) that smoking marijuana was illegal in a region in which you were smoking it. Rather, the questioner has set you up to answer in a manner that potentially incriminates you. If you answered with, "In North Dakota in 2000," you save this questioner a lot of logical and legal work. If the questioner knew you were arrested for smoking marijuana at least once and if you knew the questioner had this information, the question would be direct rather than leading.

Pierre Trudeau, a former Prime Minister of Canada, was once asked during a televised interview: "Have you ever smoked marijuana?" He answered this leading probe in this clever and witty manner: "In a country where it is legal or illegal?" Leading questions need not be hostile or incriminating. A friend might ask: "When is the last time, you went skiing in Utah?" Your friend may assume you have been skiing in Utah on at least one prior occasion. If you have been, you might answer the leading question, which here becomes a sort of shot-cut to an answer, with: "December of 1999." If you have never skied in Utah, you might reply: "Since I never skied in Utah and hear the skiing is great there, I would like to go this year." Leading questions assume a fact or event has taken place. The fact or event need be neither dastardly nor illegal. It can be benign: "When is the last time you had a relaxing weekend at the beach in Hawaii?" As long as I do not know you have ever had a relaxing weekend on the beach in Hawaii, the question leads you. If you and I both know that you have had at least one relaxing weekend at the beach in Hawaii, my question would not be leading. It would be a direct question.

Leading questions and imperatives that used highly emotive language, especially emotive language that inflames or defames, are called *loaded.* Leading questions and imperatives that are loaded capitalize on tricky, biased, and emotionally charged diction. These questions are loaded: "When will you escape from your diabolical boss at that hellish company that enslaves you?" or "Who is the 'road-kill' I saw you throwing yourself at in that sleazy tavern on Friday?' The imperative forms of these questions are: "Tell me (or Please tell me) when you will escape from you diabolic boss at that hellish company that enslaves you" and "Tell me (or Please tell me) who the 'road-kill' I saw you throwing yourself at was in that sleazy tavern on Friday." Both questions use anything but neutral language. Both aim to snarl, incite, inflame, and otherwise demean a situation through word choice. In the rational discourse of argumentation, the aim of the language employed is to be as fair, descriptive, neutral, and free of bias as possible. While biased language can be openly discussed, it would be discussed through metalanguage, metamessage, or metacommunication alone (DeVito, *Human Communication*, 2003, pp. 7 & G9).

General Language Analysis

Information on language is necessary for success in general argumentation. The language concepts that are selected here come primarily from semantics and semiotics – especially practical matters pertaining to grammar and style. Broad and applied concerns addressed in language studies must be addressed in any communication act as verbally sensitive and verbally dependent as argumentation.

Several concepts for analyzing language will be explained. These terms become a part of our metalanguage: that is, language about language. We shall use these terms dealing with argumentation as part of our meta-argumentation or argumentative language about argumentation. The topics include: extensional and intensional orientation, dating, indexing, definition, modal auxiliary and signal verbs, either/or terms, snarl and purr words, *is* vs. ought confusions, *is* and its several uses, ambiguous use of *can* and *able*, limited vs. layered meanings, technical vs. ordinary language terms, denotation, connotation, levels of abstraction, literal vs. figurative language, parts of speech analysis, and sexist language (Fiordo, 1977; Fiordo, 1990, pp. 10-15; Engel, 2000, pp. 60-87; Jensen, 1980, pp. 277-93; DeVito, 2003, pp. 120-29 & 310-11; Hodges et al, 2001). Language analysis constitutes a course in itself. Our account here will assist you in the construction, demolition (or deconstruction), and acceptance of statements, proofs, and the arguer's ethos. But, our account only serves introductory purposes and is not thorough. You will have here but a sketch of the importance and function of language in argumentation. You are encouraged to pursue advanced language studies.

An orientation that is *extensional* relies on records, evidence, and facts as well as observation and verification of events through the senses and technological extensions of the senses: for example, heat-sensing lenses, microscopes, telescopes, seismographs, audiometers, EEGs, and the like. An orientation that is *intensional* relies on words and is highly verbal with little or no reliance on the senses. Discussing the verifiable, external, empirical world with extreme reliance on the verbal and with little or no reliance on observation would constitute an intensional orientation. When we orient ourselves extensionally, we check our words, ideas, images, and thoughts of reality or the outside world against what we can observe and verify. When we orient ourselves intensionally, we rely on the notions inside our heads without checking them against reality or the outside world. These concepts come from the literature on general semantics. This discipline of language analysis promotes the idea that the ways of science or the extensional orientation constitute the ways of sanity. The extreme form of the intensional orientation does not constitute the ways of sanity; rather, they constitute the ways of "un-sanity." As symbol using creatures, while we are a blend of both, we should strive to be predominantly extensional for our own mental, social, and communicative health.

For example, two people can argue about the salary of one of their co-workers. One can argue that this co-worker is paid too much, and the other may hold that this co-worker is paid too little. Although neither may know how much the co-worker makes, both may argue without resolving this conflict if they are intensionally oriented. However, if one suggests that they find out how much the co-worker actually earns, there may be a decision to look into the records. If an open-records policy prevails, the disputants may check the pay record, learn what the co-worker actually makes, and decide at that point whether to continue their deliberations or not. However, they have left an intensional orientation for an extensional orientation. This occurs repeatedly in scientific endeavors. One researcher may assert that Amerindians came to what are now called the Americas through the islands of the South Pacific as well as along the Being Strait. To resolve the conflict, another researcher, one with an extensional orientation, would ask for hard evidence of this: perhaps, proof through a record of fossils and artifacts. Forensic medicine investigators who are extensionally oriented proceed in a similar fashion in reconstructing the scene and history of a crime.

The language concepts of *dating* and *indexing* add to the empirical analysis of language that can benefit those involved in a dispute or inquiry, a fight or a dialogue. Dating and indexing recognize the uniqueness of people, things, and events in the physical world and the lack of uniqueness available

49

to us through everyday discourse. Someone can declare that "Michael Jackson is a decent human being." Dating would put a time on Michael Jackson, such as "Michael Jackson in 1985," and in doing so would minimize controversy with those who might be thinking of the allegations against him at a later date. Indexing would point a finger at the unique being of Michael Jackson. It might take the form of an appositive, such as "Michael Jackson, the well-known rock singer, entertainer, and recording-artist." Indexing, in a sense, identifies someone through a number, such a social security number, so that no one confuses Michael Jackson #902-10-1234 with Michael Jackson #911-22-1812.

Included in the contributions from general semantics is the notion of levels of abstraction. Each word has a reference; that is, something referred to, denoted, designated, or signified. Some words are concrete and specific while others are abstract and general. The *level of abstraction* refers to the degree on a continuum that a word is concrete or abstract. Words that are comparatively concrete are seen as being low in abstraction while words that are comparatively abstract are seen as being high in abstraction. "Collie" refers to a concrete noun and is subsequently seen as being low in abstraction; "Daoism refers to an abstract noun and is subsequently seen as being high in abstraction. "Collie" is a part of the empirical world, but "Daoism" is a part of the ideational world. A collie has existence *in re*, but the dao has existence *in intellectu* (Fiordo, 1990, p. 10).

Abstraction, in short, refers to the "process through symbolization of leaving out details," a process that "usually proceeds from lower to higher levels." Hayakawa warned that high-level abstraction is commonly exploited to confuse people. As a safeguard, he suggested we ground ourselves in the low-level abstraction of extensional (namely, empirical) experience so that we do not get lost in the verbal quandaries of high-level, intensional, mental abstraction. He also advised that we blend high-level with low-level abstractions so that we do not become guilty of dead-level abstraction: that is, being stuck in a realm of too many concrete or too many abstract words.

To illustrate the process of abstraction, at the bottom level of abstraction is the process level. If we use the TV canine hero "Lassie" as an example, "Lassie" is the lowest level of abstraction at the verbal level of being a singular dog. However, there is Lassie at the object level; this is the level at which we see with our eyes or touch with our hands the canine known as "Lassie." "Lassie" is the name for the object we see and feel as the special dog with this name. Also, there is a level below the object level that entails the process of Lassie as a dog. This level is the one known to science: atoms, electrons, and so forth. Higher in abstraction from "Lassie" is the word "dog." Above "dog" in abstraction would be "pet." Beyond "pet" would be "animal." And, higher than the word "animal" would be the word "entity." Specific and concrete details are lost as we go up in abstraction (Fiordo,

1990, pp. 12-13). When deliberating, we should attend to the level of abstraction to make sure that what we agree about in the abstract remains acceptable when applied to concrete cases.

One contribution to language analysis comes from Kenneth Burke, the American critic and rhetorician. Burke explains terministic screens and the social-political versus transcendental uses of terms (Fiordo, 1978). Language tends, according to Burke, to screen out many items while focusing on those features receiving our attention through the term we use. So, if someone describes the city of Nagasaki in Japan as "charming," then our attention goes to all those meanings associated with the word *charming*. The term *charming* serves as a screen through which we perceive and interpret the city of Nagasaki. If someone described the city of Nagasaki through others terms, such as "cosmopolitan," "traditional" or "coastal," then these terms would inspirit our perception of Nagasaki. The terms screen some perception out while letting other perceptions in. For example, when we use the word "charming," words suggesting that something is not charming are screened out. See the window below:

> Charming/Non-charming.................................

An alternative, but related, way of viewing terms might deal with the idea of "lenses" instead of "screens." The notion of a "terministic screen" can also be alternated with the notion of a "terministic lens." A terministic lens can help us see by comparison through the different eyeglasses. For clear vision, if we need lenses for myopia and myopia alone, then we will not see clearly through lenses for astigmatism. Different words are like different lenses. One word, like a lens suited for the task, might give us clear vision while another word, like a lens ill-suited for the task, might blur our vision. We might be wise to select a verbal lens with respect to clarity of vision and avoid those that blur vision.

Burke also assists us in making a distinction between discourse that is primarily socio-political and primarily transcendental. Terminology that entails police and legal efforts deals with the socio-political level of language. We encounter words like *arraigned, precinct, class action suit, plea bargaining, grand jury, manslaughter*, and so on. Terminology that entails spiritual and intellectual matters deals with the transcendental level of language. We encounter words like *negative capability, satori, the beatific vision, the Dao, the Dharma, Communion with the Holy Spirit, Prana, wholism*, and so on. When expressing disagreement or calling attention to differences, discourse that prevails at either of these levels would provide insight to the advocates or inquirers about the powers and limits of those involved in the discussion. One person may reflect strength in socio-emotional discourse with weakness in transcendental discourse; another may reverse these and be strong in transcendental concepts but weak in socio-emotional ones.

Defining terms is a complex activity with numerous classifications. Different textbook writers will offer varied typologies for definitions. We are selecting several types that occur frequently: dictionary, stipulation, and operational. A dictionary definition is found in general and special dictionaries that are published by reputable sources: for example, Merriam-Webster, Random House, Oxford English Dictionary, Black's Law Dictionary, and so on. For example, the *Merriam-Webster Unabridged Dictionary* for 2002 defines the word *alibi* as "(1) the plea of having been at the time of the commission of an act elsewhere than at the place of commission; also, the fact or state of having been elsewhere at the time; (2) an excuse usually intended to avert blame or punishment (as for failure or negligence)." A dictionary definition may also entail the etymology of a word to explain it. To stipulate a definition is to provide a definition for a term as a speaker or writer will be using it in the context of their discourse. It takes the form of explaining terms in this manner: (1) "For our purposes, *freedom* means doing what we want to do while *happiness* means doing what we like to do"; (2) "In our context, a *comedian* is someone who says funny things while a *comic* is someone who says things in a funny manner."

Word meanings are more complex than they may appear to be at a glance. A word's denotation and connotation must be considered with special care when facing controversial issues. The *denotation* refers to the literal definition of a term; the *connotation* refers to the social and emotional associations of a term. *Purr* and *snarl* words have high connotations. Purr words have favorable associations, and snarl words have unfavorable associations. To describe a colleague by the names "gem" and "jewel" would be terms likely used as purr words; to describe a colleague by the names "leech" and "slob" would be terms likely used as snarl words. Both would be highly connotative. Their denotation would be low in comparison. A neutral term might be simply "colleague." A parent may refer to a girl standing next to him or her as "daughter." *Daughter* might denote a female biological offspring; it might connote such terms as "my premium child," "my little angel," "my pumpkin," and other endearing purr words.

Literal and figurative uses of words play significant roles also in communication and argumentation. Literal use of a term is close to the designation of a dictionary definition. Figurative use of a term is any comparative extension of a term. So, to refer to a girl standing next to someone as his or her "daughter" might carry the literal meaning of a female biological offspring. To describe the same person figuratively as a "daughter" would mean the girl is of or like a daughter but not actually so. Much discourse has been spent on the meaning of the story in *Genesis* of Adam and Eve. What does this story mean in the context of this scripture? Was it meant literally or figuratively?

Meanings can also be multiple or limited. To expect one word to have one meaning and one meaning only is not likely possible. One special word, however, can have limited meaning because the term is used neither frequently nor broadly. Some semanticists refer to the goal of having one word mean only one thing as the one-word-one-meaning fallacy, as with Hayakawa's (1990) view in *Language in Thought and Action*. Math and science may hold this up as a goal to strive for but always fall short of in daily use. Yet, a word like *triangle* can have a limited use in geometry as a word like *mother* can have a limited use in chemistry. In literary arts, especially poetry, oftentimes the goal is opposite that of math and science. The goal is to have polysemy or pluri-signification: that is, words with rich, multiple meanings and associations. Poetic discourse may be interested in layers of meaning. Everyday language may have multiple meanings when limited meanings are desired and vice-versa. In short, sometimes we need words with ideally one meaning or but a couple layers of meaning, and sometimes we need words with numerous layers of meaning. When disagreeing and arguing, both ends have to be noted: words with limited and multiple layers.

An operational definition explains terms by reference to a list of operations that must be performed like a recipe for cooking or mixing drinks. For example, an *urban respondent* to a questionnaire might be defined as a "respondent who lives in a Metropolitan Area as defined by the Census Bureau" (Wimmer & Dominick, 2003, p. 46). Another illustration would be this. A fitness coach may define an *aerobic workout* operationally as "jog for 30 minutes first, kayak for 30 minutes second, and walk with one kilogram weights in each hand for 30 minutes last." These actions constitute the operational definition for what the fitness coach means by an "aerobic workout." No attempt is made with an operational definition to define a term conceptually or theoretically. The operations or actions that are performed constitute the definition.

Technical and ordinary language can be appropriate, depending on the context and use. Although ordinary language is frequently preferred because it is familiar to large numbers of people, technical language can be beneficial when precision is required or desired. While a technical word like *argumentativeness* might be suitable for one audience, an ordinary phrase like *willingness to disagree constructively* might be suitable for another audience. Most professional jargon is technical and serves a beneficial role in professional contexts. However, ordinary language would be preferred in most general contexts of language use. For example, a yoga instructor may talk about *hatha yoga* or *ashtanga yoga* to yoga students but merely *yoga* or *stretching techniques* to a general audience.

Especially technical is much of the language related to computers and their programs. To make sense to those not familiar with technical language, computer technicians would have the challenge and opportunity to explain in plain English what they mean by a scanner with 1200 X 4800 dpi, 48-bit color, USB interface, and Win 98/2000/ME/XP.

A number of distinctions in language are philosophically and logically more significant that other language distinctions. Several important distinctions follow. One involves the *is-ought* controversy (Morris, 1970; Fiordo, 1977). When arguing and communicating generally, it is wise to distinguish between what is the case and what ought to be the case on any matter at hand. When we look at humanity, it is the case that we offend, hurt, and kill one another; perhaps, this ought not to be the case but it is. Or, we can say that it ought to be the case that we love our neighbor as we love ourselves. Although we may love our neighbor as ourselves on occasion, this is not always the case. Hence, we have the tension or controversy connected with what is and what ought to be.

A helpful distinction must be made between the sometimes ambiguous terms of *can* and *able*. This is drawn from the thinking of Stephen Toulmin in *The Uses of Argument*. When one says, "I can file for Canadian citizenship," it may mean that the person is legally eligible for citizenship; it may not mean this person is able to file forms to become a Canadian citizen. If one says that she or he can run a stop-sign, it might mean this act is physically possible; it may not mean the act is legally acceptable. So, can and able should be distinguished for practical purposes when arguing.

Due to their ability to mollify statements and minimize friction between communicators, *modals* and *signal verbs* are worthy of attention. When we use a form of the verb *to be* or active verb we make statements that are stronger than statements made using modal forms, such as *may, can, might, could, would,* and *should* (Hodges et al, 2001). These forms temper the power of the statements and change the type of proof or support that is required. Modals allow us to soften statements. For example, a philosopher might say: "Pascal's religious wager is the only intelligent view possible on God and eternal life." In this form, the statement is assertive – perhaps, too assertive. The philosopher might say instead: "Pascal's religious wager might be the only intelligent view possible on God and eternal life." In this form, the statement softens the discussion. Instead of creating the conditions for a definite counterpoint, the modal form allows the speaker and the listener less stringent and more relative grounds for deliberation. The other modal forms function similarly to reduce the assertiveness of statements when, in fact, you do not want to be so assertive or truly believe you have no basis for such assertiveness. The facts, which confuse some biased people, do not always support strong statements. When the facts do not support strong statements, then modal formulations offer us reasonable assistance.

Signal verbs allow us, likewise, to soften statements and reduce contentiousness. Signal verbs provide listeners and readers with the evaluation of material a speaker or writer discusses (Harnack & Kleppinger, 1997, Online! The Internet Guide for Students and Writers, NY: St. Martin's). Examples of signal verbs are: *has proved that, says, pontificates, argues that, estimates that, fears that, speculates that, has found that, thinks, declares, wonders if,* and so on (DeVito, 2003, p. 311). When someone declares that "Tanning beds cause cancer and are no safer than exposure to direct sunlight," the declaration is made unnecessarily and imprecisely. Rather, the same communicator can state the following with far more accuracy and care: "A recent study at John Hopkins Medical School has found that tanning beds cause cancer and are no safer than exposure to direct sunlight." Signal verbs allow us to provide feedforward on material we are about to discuss with others; they are practical and rational grammatical and rhetorical uses of language.

Using *either/or* terms can pose problems in communication in general and argumentation in particular. *Either/or* terms refer to polar opposites: that is, antonyms. Such opposites *as good/bad, right/wrong, healthy/sick, moral/immoral, pretty/ugly, true/false, angel/devil, smart/stupid,* and *saint/sinner* provide insight into "either/or" limitations in language use. One or more words can be inserted between these antonyms. To declare someone is either a "angel" or a "devil" is to ignore the enormity of people between these polar extremes. The polar usage overlooks all the blends of humanity between those who can be called "angels" and those who can be called "devils"; it also ignores the numerous terms that might suggest degrees of goodness and badness rather than these polar opposites. Individuals can be "humans" rather than "angels" or "devils." People can be smart, stupid, and numerous IQ ratings between these extremes. And, one individual can be healthy, another sick, and a third somewhere between these opposites. Oftentimes, we use words to modify the antonym classification. We might say: "She is relatively healthy" or "He is comparatively sick." We have to remain argumentatively sharp about the use of any polar terms since they frequently distort reality.

The English linking verb *is* creates a number of semantic and logical problems. We link it here with the notion of English Prime language or English without the verb *to be* in any of its forms. When someone declares, "I am an American" (or a Canadian or an Australian and so on), what is the relationship between the "I" and the "American" expressed through "is"? Since his statement may mean any of the following at least, it is ambiguous and may have to be used with more precision: (1) I have the status of being a naturalized citizen of the USA; (2) I belong to the classification of people who live in the USA; (3) I form my identity under the label "American"; and, (4) No difference exists between the individual represented by the pronoun "I" and what embodies someone called an "American." English with out the verb *to be* is illustrated in my translations of "I am an American" in examples 1 through 4. To minimize the damage that can follow from the multiple uses of "is," English Prime eliminates its use and substitutes active verbs that presumably will be less abstract and vague in their use.

Examining parts of speech that are used in argumentative discourse can be extremely helpful. An advocate may describe someone by using a name or an action. Nike ads have distinguished a female who "runs" from a female who is a "runner." Bill Pearl, a well-known Mr. Universe winner and author of *Keys to the Inner Universe*, once described himself as someone who "likes to lift weights" rather than as a "weightlifter" or a "bodybuilder." When we investigate the parts of speech used to provide an account, we may discover an implicit epistemology and argument. To say, along with Nike, that a certain female is "athletic" is different from declaring she is an "athlete." A noun carries different, and sometimes more demanding and formal criteria, from that attributed through an adjective or a verb. In short, to say that someone is an "athlete" rather than "athletic" is to make a claim about that person that is respectable yet less formally demanding. An adjective is less weighty here than a noun. To assert that someone "runs" instead of asserting that this person is a "runner" or to assert that someone "lifts weights" instead of asserting that this person is a "weightlifter" is respectable yet less formally demanding. Verbs are less weighty here than nouns. It is to our advantage to look closely at the part of speech that is functioning in the communicative context in general and the argumentative context in particular. During deliberation, one can distinguish in an autobiographical statement, for example, "I am athletic" without claiming to be an "athlete" or "I dance" without claiming to be a "dancer" or "I write" without claiming to be a "writer." Our nouns, adjectives, verbs, and other parts of speech must be noted routinely to present an accurate and ethical account of events.

The last item we cover under general language analysis pertains to sexist language. Sexist terms should be avoided or used at the risk of the communicator. Social consequences are not always severe, and sometimes no adverse reactions follow. We urge their elimination (or at least minimization) to respect sensitivities in daily civilized matters. English has a number of sexist expression that can be modified easily. Several are provided to provide you with a modicum of guidance. The following sexist terms can be readily modified.

Suggestions for nonsexist word choices should be made. The following words should be considered as reasonable changes from sexist to nonsexist terms: 1) mankind to *humanity, human beings,* or *people*; 2) <u>policeman/policewoman</u> to *police officer*; 3) <u>stewardess/steward</u> to *flight attendant*; 3) <u>fireman/firewoman</u> to *firefighter*; and 4) <u>wife/husband</u> *to spouse/partner.* In the context of a sentence, the following changes from sexist to nonsexist expressions are recommended: 1) "<u>He</u> (when referring to a person in general) should see <u>his</u> doctor regularly" to "*One (She or he, he or she, or s/he) should see <u>a</u> doctor regularly*"; 2) "<u>She</u> (when singular is not required and plural would be equivalent) should see <u>her</u> doctor routinely" to "<u>People</u> (or <u>We</u> or <u>You</u>) should see a doctor routinely"; and, 3) "<u>She or he</u> should see a doctor routinely" to, when possible, the imperative form of, "See a doctor routinely."

Natural, sexual differences should be noted with care. Language should accurately reflect sexual, biological differences. If this is not done the linguistic effect is absurd. Please note the following biological basis for the linguistic examples: 1) "<u>She</u> should get a medical examination in <u>her</u> second trimester of pregnancy"; 2) "<u>He</u> should get a prostate examination yearly at <u>his</u> age."

To discuss these special biological matters in neutral language would be confusing and possibly absurd. A news broadcaster, presumably attempting to explain a rape in neutral language, reported that a "women was raped by three people today one block from city hall." If three "people" raped her, the conditions embodying the rape might be different from three "Caucasian males between the age of 15 and 20" raping her. Caution must be exercised in using suitable gender and sex language and unsuitable sexist language.

The use of heterosexist or homophobic language also has limitations. Heterosexist language refers to "language used to disparage gay men and lesbians" (DeVito, 2003, p. 121 & 124). When someone presumes an individual is heterosexual because the majority of the population is heterosexual, that person denies to some degree the identity and legitimacy of gay men and lesbians. A homophobic person may eschew the possibility of the individual before her or him being anything but heterosexual. For example, heterosexist language might be used to offend gay men and lesbians when used in the following ways: To refer to a "gay professor," a "lesbian doctor," a "gay actor," or a "lesbian athlete," and so on is to highlight the affectional orientation of the person in a context where it may not be relevant. To compliment gay men and lesbians by saying "they don't look it" is no complement to someone who is not heterosexual. To praise the appearance of gay men and lesbians by saying "What a Waste!" is far more an insult than a compliment. In referring to "John Doe" or "Jane Doe" is to be heterosexist as well since a neutral name, such as "Jade Doe" or "Chris Doe" or "Pat Doe," will accomplish the same end without being heterosexist.

Because of its cultural significance and critical acceptance in communication studies, feminist contributions to theories of language, communication, and argumentation are introduced. Due to its scholarly richness, Stephen Littlejohn's account of feminism in communication studies will serve as a guide in this text. Starting with feminist philosophies and theories, Littlejohn summarizes feminist criticism, standpoint theories, liberal feminism, radical feminism, sexist language, and the relationship between sexism and power. Littlejohn (2002) explains that feminism is a diversified and complex system of thought, not a single theory. Feminist theorists have noted that many aspects of life are experienced with respect to the masculine and the feminine: that is they are "gendered." Feminist theorists assume that gender constitutes a "pervasive category of experience," is a useful "social construction" that has been "dominated by a male bias" that is especially "oppressive to women," and directs research in a male-biased direction that is misleading and dangerous because traditional research tends to "mute the experience of women and hide the values of women's experience" (p. 222). Furthermore, feminist theorists maintain that women have "their own form of expression" that lies "outside the dominant male system" of communication forms. Despite the fact that they are not seen as significant by the masculine world, communication forms that women have created and used have "value in their own right." One feminist theorist, Cheris Kramarae, argues that women take control of their lives and their worlds by creating communication forms that enhance communication comfort and hospitableness (p. 225).

One significant and useful addition to rhetorical and argumentation theory comes from the feminist notion of *enfoldment*. To want to change others assumes superiority and violates the values of those we are trying to change. So, instead of trying to change others, we should try to enfold others. *Enfoldment* is a term that suggests how people should communicate with each other, for to *enfold* is to "make oneself available." By enfolding, we invite others to share, offer a view to others, and listen to others. Through enfoldment, we try to understand others because, as the feminists argue on this point, change only happens when people are ready, choose to change, and external conditions are right.

Subsequently, in light of enfoldment, we should, according to Gearhart, communicate in this manner utilizing six components of enfoldment: 1) acknowledgement or listening carefully and then stating what you determine is important to others; 2) common ground or searching for and talking about common beliefs and values upon which to build; 3) mutually sharing perspectives or listening with sincere curiosity to learn more while offering an idea as a perspective rather than as a superior truth; 4) willingness to yield or being open to change a point of view held; 5) witnessing or being observationally present to show that the presentations of others are being taken seriously; and, 6) asking permission to share or inquiring into whether others are interested in hearing one's ideas.

Consequently, instead of using traditional methods in which we prepare to engage for conflict by gathering your strongest arguments to change the ideas of the others, we employ an invitational rhetoric with an attitude of enfoldment. In this case, we listen for the wisdom of the others, acknowledge the expressed viewpoint, look for common ground, invite others into of discussion to determine what we share, and finally ask permission to share our views as possible alternatives. In doing so, we open ourselves to possible change that we embrace if it is appropriate. We also feel good about the communication, understanding others better, and gaining insights we might not previously have had (p. 228).

For additional information on feminist perspectives, you are invited to read: (1) Carol Gilligan's *In a Different Voice*; (2) Karen A. Foss, Sonja K. Foss, and Cindy L. Griffin's *Feminist Rhetorical Theories*; (3) Cheris Kramarae's *Men and Women Speaking: Frameworks for Analysis; (4)* the journal *Feminist Media Studies; (5) Feminist Jurisprudence* by Mary Becker and others; and, Judith Lorber's *Gender Inequality: Feminist Theories and Politics*.

REFLECTIONS: Agreements, Conflicts, and Questions

When people argue angrily, they tend to toss words about carelessly. In contrast, language in reasonable argumentation should be examined carefully. Who bothers to distinguish propositions from questions? Who should bother to distinguish between questions suitable for debate and suitable for discussion? What practical use could be served by distinguishing propositions of fact, value, and policy? Are not all questions, in a sense, leading? Why would it be of any practical importance to determine whether a question is open or closed, direct or leading? Is there any similarity between what lawyers call an argumentative question and a leading question?

All language is loaded, is it not? English does not have the masculine and feminine endings of some languages, like Spanish and Italian. How can English be sexist? What is wrong with using a word like "mankind" and "man" generically anyway? Does feminism apply to women only? Has feminism made worthwhile contributions to American life? Should feminism be seen as making favorable contributions to society for women only or for both men and women? Is there a masculinism that parallels feminism? Does radical feminism suggest objectives that are unrealistic and impractical? Does liberal feminism simply serve the traditional masculine prejudices of contemporary society?

CHAPTER THREE
Arguments: Analysis and Evaluation

Lesson Objectives:

To provide an overview of arguments and fallacies
To offer criteria for evaluating arguments
To survey the Toulmin model of argument
To examine argumentation in a legal context

Arguments: An Overview of their Meaning, Language, and Validity

Dr. Jack Andrews, a psychologist at the University of Calgary, is pursuing research that addresses problems pertaining to clinical judgment in psychology (Personal Interview, 25 November 11). One significant theme that runs through his book has implications for judgment in general and judgment in diverse learned contexts: courts of law, schools, universities, governmental agencies, and other professional arenas. The theme of merit to argumentation in general as well as argumentation in particular contexts pertains to the making of judgments. Since bias, prejudice, confusion, ignorance, and other problems that limit the powers of rational judgment are a part of the making of judgments in everyday life, it is safer to assume that those who make judgments must marshal all within their power to minimize irrelevant and irrational factors that contribute to faulty and harmful judgments being delivered. Rather than assume that the making of judgments is plain, simple, valid, and reliable, he urges us to proceed from the ground that making judgments is difficult and challenging. The wise judgment is reached only with rigorous care; failing to reach a wise judgment is readily predictable if rational guides are not exercised with intellectual zeal. Those receiving the foolish judgment are those who suffer.

Similar to the triad from general semantics of judgment, inference, and report, Andrews suggests that judgments follow from interpretations that are reasonable and evidence that is solid. He urges that we avoid a "rush to judgment." Instead, he prescribes that anyone serving as a judge precedes a judgment with a scrutiny of facts that constitute evidence and of interpretations that are inferred from the evidence. Andrews uses the term "evidence" in a manner similar to the way general semanticists employ the term "reports" (that is, observable or verifiable facts); he uses the term "interpretation" in a manner similar to the way general semanticists employ the term "inference" (that is, a statement about the unknown made on the basis of what is known). The term judgment is used more or less interchangeably as an evaluation – preferably one derived from sound interpretation or inference and based on solid evidence or facts. He cautions that what may too frequently happen is that someone rendering a judgment fails to examine evidence carefully and rationalizes an interpretation hastily. Instead of making haste slowly to make a judgment, there is a rush to judgment without scrutinizing the evidence and interpretation of the evidence. We should consider this sage caution and method proposed by Andrews when reaching conclusions and judgments through argumentation. We cannot be too reasonable about serious matters of judgment. The more serious the matter, the more reasonable should be the analysis. Judging whether to dine on lobster or steak would not ordinarily count as a serious matter of judgment unless of course one had an allergy for lobster and not for steak.

The Mencken Measure: A Cautionary Tale for Arguing

Lockney (1986), a legal scholar and judge, makes a point based on a statement from H.L. Mencken that is relevant to argumentative criticism. More than familiar with complex legal questions for which the public craves facile answers, Lockney proposes a practical consideration of Mencken's ironic wisdom on expecting simple answers to complex questions. Reportedly, Mencken remarked that for "every complex problem, there is usually a simple answer – and usually it's wrong." A more severe version of this insightful perspective is that "every complex problem has a simple solution, and it is wrong" (p. 30). Whether we take a hard or soft position on Mencken's conclusion, we will have a critical edge over our critical competitors. If we see every complex problem as having (or usually having) a simple answer that is wrong (or usually wrong), we are sufficiently admonished to argue and solve problems with astute care.

For our critical advantage, let us consider a matter in a specific legal context of search and seizure rules. Search and seizure rules involve police interpreting and enforcing law. Critical legal scholars may to some extent "find legal rules hopelessly or unavoidably indeterminate." For example, rules of search and seizure in North Dakota may, according to Lockney, be "so confusing and indeterminate that they are unable to serve as meaningful guides to police conduct"; they are "rules that cannot be stated with sufficient clarity or detail to provide the officers adequate advance guidance" (p. 32). Indeed, as Lockney (1996) sees it, the "United States Supreme Court has struggled mightily for years to define or articulate the bounds of probable cause, the level of certainty required for a garden variety of search and seizure" (p. 970). The potential to recognize complexity should be actualized since the complexity is usually there.

Returning to Mencken's measure or rule, what we desire is a simple answer to a complex question, but a simple solution is not usually correct. What appears to have a plain solution to a complex problem can predictably be wrong. Since the rules may be indeterminate to a degree, complex answers should be sought for questions that delude us into thinking there are simple answers. When simple answers are desired for complex problems, it does not mean that simple answers are possible. The argumentative critic pursues a realistic answer to a complex problem.

Analyzing Reasoning

The thought of S. Morris Engel (2000) on logic, language, and informal fallacies serves as the primary ground for analyzing and evaluating legitimate, fallacious, and sophistic arguments in this course. Engel's sees an argument as a "piece of reasoning in which one or more statements are offered as support for some other statement." The statement we support is the argument's *conclusion* while the reasons we give to support the conclusion are the *premises* (pp.7-8). If we make a claim or state a conclusion but give no reason for others to believe it, we have made no argument. An argument's purpose is to get another to agree with us. When we argue, we take something that is not known generally nor agreed upon and try to establish that it is a fact. That is, an argument endeavors to prove through supporting reasons that a statement in question is true. In contrast, an explanation (again, not an argument) merely elaborates on a claim or statement it assumes to be true (pp.10-12).

To study arguments, we must study fallacies or unsound arguments. In this course, we cover generally informal fallacies rather than formal fallacies. A course in logic formal logic would serve you well on formal fallacies in arguments. "Informal fallacies," Engel tells us, are "unsound in their content, as opposed to their form or structure." Engel's teachings on informal fallacies include fallacies of ambiguity, presumption, and relevance. A logical argument should always answer these three questions: (1) Is the assertion of the argument *clear*? (2) Are the facts in the argument *correctly represented*? (3) Is the reasoning in the argument *valid or strong*? Fallacies of ambiguity direct our critical attention to arguments that fail to meet the challenge of the first question: Is the argument *clear*? Fallacies of presumption direct our critical attention to arguments that fail to meet the challenge of the second question: Is the argument *true*? And, fallacies of relevance direct our critical attention to arguments that fail to meet the challenge of the third question: Is the argument *valid*? In other words, fallacies of ambiguity signal unsound arguments because they use words that, either singly or in combination, can be understood in more than one way in a given context. Fallacies of presumption signal unsound arguments because they have unfounded or unproven assumptions embedded in them. And, fallacies of relevance signal unsound arguments because the premises, despite appearances, do not support the conclusion drawn in the argument (pp. 94-95, 99, 143, and 213). A memorable acronym to assist your learning of these three classification of fallacies is PAR: presumption, ambiguity, and relevance. And, that is about par for this wordy discipline.

Engel's (2000) text details numerous fallacies: too many to include in this context. Ten are selected for exposition here. For the complete list, see the Engel's text dealing with the fallacies of ambiguity on pages 99-101, the fallacies of presumption on pages 143-146, and the fallacies of relevance on pages 213-215. The fallacies we examine directly include: equivocation, division, accent, either/or, hasty generalization, false cause, slippery slope, genetic fallacy, appeal to ignorance, and *tu quoque*.

Fallacies of ambiguity follow. A fallacy of equivocation entails an "ambiguity caused by a shift between two legitimate meanings of a term." For example, "If you believe in the miracles of science, you should also believe in the miracles of the Bible." A fallacy of division involves the assumption that what is true of the whole or the group must be true of the parts or the members. For example, "Since this is the richest sorority on campus, Celine, a member of this sorority, must therefore be one of the richest sorority sisters on campus." The fallacy of division is the reverse of the fallacy of composition in which there is an assumption that what is true of a part of a whole or a member of a group has to be true of the whole or the group. For example, "Since Nicolin is the tallest player on his soccer team in this school district, the soccer team must have the tallest players in the school district." The fallacy of accent results from a statement uttered with an uncertain tone of voice, uttered with an unclear stress in the tone of voice, or quoted out of context. For example, if vocalized with harsh or gentle emphasis, "You shall not steal" and "You shall not steal" illustrate the tone and stress parts of the fallacy. However, the quotation out of context that is part of this fallacy can be seen in this example: "Abe Lincoln was not the President it is thought he was because he said, 'You can fool all of the people some of the time" (p. 100).

Fallacies of presumption are next. Either/or fallacies (also known as false dilemmas, black-and-white fallacies, and fallacies of bifurcation) treat a distinction as exhaustive when other alternatives exist. For example, "You're either with us or against us." Hasty generalization fallacies use "insufficient evidence or an isolated example as the basis for a widely general conclusion." For

64

example, "I had a bad experience with my former boss, and from that I learned that all bosses are oppressive." Fallacies of false cause "infer a causal link between two events when no such causal connection has been established." For example, "Sales went up after we instituted our recent advertising campaign, so the success of our campaign is obvious." Slippery slope fallacies assume, "unjustifiably, that a proposed step will set off an undesirable and uncontrollable chain of events." For example, "Today, we endorse abortion, but tomorrow it will be euthanasia of the mentally ill, and then the infirm, the aged, or anyone else considered undesirable" (pp. 145-146).

Fallacies of relevance are the last to be covered. Genetic fallacies attack a "thesis, institution, or idea by condemning its background or origin." For example, "Australia will never be truly decent, for look at the convicts who developed it." Fallacious appeals to ignorance emphasize "not the evidence for a thesis but the lack of evidence against it." For example, "There has to be extraterrestial life since no one has proven there is not." And, lastly, *tu quoque* fallacies attempt to establish that an "opponent does not act in accord with his or her thesis." For example, "What right does my doctor have to advise me to go on a diet to lose weight when she herself is obese?" (p. 214)

According to Eisenberg and Ilardo (1972), exposing a fallacy is a delicate art that calls for "keen observation, infallible timing, and indefatigable effort." Knowing about fallacies is a first step only. You must work on the delicate art of exposing the fallacy. To these authors, a *fallacy* is a "deceptive or misleading tactic used intentionally or accidentally by an advocate" and may have the "effect of deluding an opponent or an onlooker" (p. 55). Read pages 55 to 71 from Eisenberg and Ilardo for their complete list of fallacies. They discuss 26 frequently occurring fallacies and caution us on their use. Three fallacies they demonstrate in their text will be presented next: the *argumentum ad populum* fallacy, the *post hoc ergo propter hoc* (or, the *post hoc*) fallacy), and the fallacy of untouchable authority.

In the *argumentum ad populum* fallacy, the fallacy is to be found in the view that "something is true because so many people believe it." This fallacy appeals to "popular opinions and prejudices": an assertion such as "10 million Americans cannot be wrong." History provides numerous cases of new ideas being attacked because most people held older ideas that were faulty. For example, Galileo suffered because others at his time believed his ideas were absurd and blasphemous. So, when an advocate seeks support for a view based solely on its acceptance by popular opinion, that advocate stands on thin ice. An illustration of this fallacy can be discerned in the following dialog:

Believer: There is no doubt in my mind that God exists.

Unbeliever: Do you have any proof that God exists?

Believer: Yes, personal proof. God has made His presence known to me.

Unbeliever: That is not proof to me. Do you have any other more persuasive evidence?

Believer: Yes, the fact that millions of people all over the world agree with me that God exists (p. 60).

In the *post hoc ergo propter hoc* or *post hoc* fallacy, the fallacy to be found derives from faulty causal reasoning. This fallacy means "after the fact, therefore, because of the fact." The arguer asserts that "because one thing precedes another in time and space, it causes the second to occur." For example, because church bells rang and ten minutes later it snowed, it is concluded that the church bells caused it to snow. I use the *post hoc* fallacy as a slightly different attribution of faulty causation from the fallacy of false cause Engel discusses. I use Engel's false cause to indicate problems related to distinguishing between correlation and causation: distinctions difficult even for scientists to make under some circumstances. To return to the fallacy called *post hoc*, an illustration of this fallacy can be discerned in the following dialog:

Ingrid: I couldn't start my car this morning.

Paolo: Why are you telling me?

Ingrid: Because you used it last.

Paolo: And, just what is that supposed to mean?

Ingrid: Nothing, except that it was fine until you drove it.

Paolo: Are you suggesting that because I used your old car yesterday and it wouldn't start this morning that I was responsible?

Ingrid: It certainly makes sense. You were the last one to use it, therefore…(p. 58).

In the <u>fallacy of untouchable authority</u>, the fallacy is to be found when it is held that people in official roles should be exempt from criticism. Criticism is avoided or even prohibited. Eisenberg and Ilardo explain that this is "a somewhat backward approach to respect for authority." Rather, "respect should follow the establishment of honesty and integrity." They tell us that "we ought to allow all reasonable criticisms against such established agencies as the government, the church, and the university to be made." An illustration of this fallacy can be discerned in the following dialog:

Terry: Have you heard *The North Dakota Tribune's* charges of corruption against the police commissioner?

Jerry: Yes, and I think it's a disgrace!

Terry: A disgrace? Why?

Jerry: Because by charging her with corruption, the *Tribune* is casting aspersions on the character of the whole police force. A breakdown in respect for the police department is sure to follow (p. 71).

      Three fallacies pertaining to statistical evidence will be mentioned. Since statistics form a common part of modern discourse and mass media reporting, statistical fallacies can creep in undetected. Sprague and Stuart (2006) elaborate three statistical fallacies that would be of benefit here: the fallacy of the average, the fallacy of the unknown base, and the fallacy of the atypical (or arbitrary) time frame. While we may recognize that language is ambiguous, we may not think of numbers as being ambiguous. The fallacy of the average calls our attention to numbers that are at odds with facts. For example, a company may use an arithmetic mean or "average of 6 computer scanners per department when, if fact, the marketing department has 40 scanners, and most other departments have 1 or none." Clearly, the arithmetic mean is not suitable when one or two extremes distort the distribution. The median or mode might be more valid and less distorting in this situation (pp. 79-80). With the fallacy of the unknown base, an arguer gives the "mistaken impression that a large population has been sampled" when the evidence was unscientific or slim. For example, "Two out of three mechanics recommend this synthetic oil" when in fact only three mechanics were polled (p. 80). The fallacy of the atypical (or arbitrary) time frame misleads by treating something as typical when it is not. For example, a computer company claims that sales in February were double those of January. Unless we know that January is the worst month for the computer industry, this statistical claim would distort the true and contextual significance of the sales increase (Ibid). In short, the increase was atypical, not typical. There is little reason to be favorably impressed.

      Freeley (1986) provides us with a view of fallacies that is consistent with Engel as well as with Eisengberg and Ilardo. He warns us that our task in argumentation is not merely to "name the fallacy but to be able to demonstrate to those who render the decision how or why the matter in question is fallacious." This chore is easier said than done because fallacies are "often field dependent" and therefore "must be considered in context." Consequently, fallacies are contextualized: that is, an argument may be fallacious in specified contexts rather than intrinsically fallacious (p. 153). With this distinction noted, Freeley provides us with an alternative version of argumentative analysis. He sets forth selected fallacies that you will find useful: namely, fallacies dealing with evidence, fallacies dealing with reasoning (example, analogy, cause, and sign), fallacies dealing with language (ambiguity, verbalism, loaded language, and grammatical structure), and fallacies dealing with pseudo-arguments (extension, arguing in a circle, ignoring an issue, baiting an opponent, repeated assertion, structured response, special pleading, substitution the person for the argument, substituting bombast for argument, denying a valid conclusion, popular appeal, straw argument, appeal to ignorance, pseudo-questions, appeal to tradition, non sequitur, and post hoc) that you will find useful (pp. 152-163). You should read him thoroughly for his insight into argumentative obstacles to valid and clear thinking and communicating (See Freeley, pp. 152-163).

Two major contributions to overall argumentation evaluation from Infante will be reviewed. They cover the content and the relationship components of argumentation. All position speeches should be assessed on these two fundamental grounds: (1) refutation of oppositional positions or arguments and construction of your own position against the oppositional positions or arguments (the content or logical component), and (2) the interpersonal relations you develop during the position speech (the relational or socio-emotional component). The appraisal criteria from Infante (1988, pp. 45-54 and 69-80) are provided and advised.

You are invited to follow these guidelines from Infante in establishing the logical or content component of your position speeches (pp. 69-80):

1. Summarize the argument to be refuted.
2. Give an overview of your objections to the argument.
3. Attack the evidence presented in the argument.
    Is the evidence recent enough?
    Was enough evidence presented?
    Is the evidence from a reliable source?
    Is the evidence consistent with known facts?
    Can the evidence be interpreted in other ways?
    Is the evidence directly relevant to the claim?
4. Attack the reasoning presented in the argument.
    Were any important assumptions unproven?
    Were there inconsistencies in reasoning?
    Were arguments about cause valid?

Were comparisons based on things that are not equal?

Was reasoning from signs valid?

Were emotional appeals used instead of sound reasoning?

5. Summarize your refutation.

6. Explain how your refutation weakens your opponent's position.

You are invited to follow these guidelines from Infante (1988) for managing the socio-emotional or relational component of position speeches (p. 45):

1. Does the argument test ideas, not people?

2. Are the principles of argumentation used with compassion?

3. Is the opponent's sense of competence reaffirmed?

4. Are the opponents allowed to finish what they are saying?

5. Do the arguers emphasize equality?

6. Do the arguers emphasize shared attitudes?

7. Do the arguers show they are interested in one another's views?

8. Do the arguers use a calm or somewhat subdued delivery?

9. Do the arguers control the pace of the argument?

10. Do the arguers allow their opponents to save face?

You are also urged to use Infante's system of invention by proposing a plan in response to a controversial question and then supporting the proposal with reasoning and evidence. Note well that you must respect the content and the relational components always. Position speeches must attack opposing positions to deal with resistance to your ideas through persuasion or by inviting transformation. Resistance to positions taken in a speech might be done in a summary manner so that the stress can be placed on constructing a positive position.

Infante's System of Invention

Based on Infante's system of invention, position speeches might take this form and respond to these questions:

Issues (major ones) and sub-issues stated as discussion (or a debate) questions of fact, value, or policy [For example, Should American homeland security be increased? (question of policy for debate); What should the American policy on homeland security be? (question of policy for discussion)]:

Problem

What are the signs of a problem?

What is the specific harm?

How widespread is the harm?

Blame

What causes the problem?

Is the present system at fault?

Should the present system be changed?

Solution

What are the best possible solutions?

Which solution best serves the problem?

Consequences

What good outcomes will result form the solution?

What bad outcomes will result from the solution? (pp. 45-54)

Another model for evaluating argumentation involves a system for generating argumentation in general but especially argumentation for forensic purposes. In light of our litigious American society, the Toulmin model of argument, developed by the argumentation philosopher Stephen Toulmin, must be examined. The crucial terms in this model are: *data, warrant,* and *claim.* Additional critical terms include: *qualifier, backing,* and *rebuttal.* The exposition on Toulmin will be drawn from Matlon's (1988) text entitled *Communication in the Legal Process* (pp. 83-86). Matlon performs the service of applying the terminology from the Toulmin model of argument in general and legal argument in particular to several legitimate arguments: namely, arguments from cause, sign, analogy, and authority. The *claim* is the argumentative conclusion, statement, position, or point of view. The *data* are the facts, information, or grounds for your argument. The *warrant* is the bridge or inference of the argument. The warrant justifies how you move from data to claim. The *qualifier* limits the claim. Such words as "possibly," "probably," and "likely" are typical qualifiers; such legal phrases as "according to the preponderance of evidence standard" or "according to the beyond a reasonable doubt standard" are also qualifiers. The *reservation* is the rebuttal or the circumstances under which the <u>claim</u> may not be valid or may not apply. The word "unless" typically signals a reservation. The final concept is backing. *Backing* is the part of the argument that "provides authority or support for the warrant."

To illustrate this, the following example is based on one Malton offers:

Ms. Alpha, an eyewitness, sees Ms. Beta enter an intersection without stopping at the stop sign (Data). A claim follows from this data: Therefore, Ms. Beta is guilty of a traffic violation (Claim) beyond any reasonable doubt (Qualifier). This claim has a warrant with backing: since failure to stop at a stop sign is unlawful (Warrant) on account of Section 123 of the Vehicle Code of the State of Dakota (Backing). Are there possible exceptions or reservations? The claim is valid and true unless there was an unequal enforcement of the law and/or Ms. Alpha is an unreliable eyewitness (Reservations) (p.84).

According to Malton, Toulmin's model applies with benefit to these arguments: cause, sign, analogy, and authority. Causal arguments show that an event is the cause or condition of another event. So, an attorney argues from cause when "in a tort case concerning negligence," the failure to repair a furnace (Data) was "a cause producing the effect of a sudden fire and explosion (Claim). Sign arguments consist of relationships between variable are so close that "the presence or absence of one is an indication of the presence or absence of the other." So, a history of exaggerating or lying (Data) might serve to prove the sign argument that the "person is doing the same thing in court today (Claim). Arguments from analogy draw from comparisons. So, attorneys argue by analogy when they cite "cases comparable to the one in litigation" (Data) and consequently advance the view that the "present case should be decided according to those precedents" (Claim). And, arguments from authority use the opinions of authorities to support a claim. So, a conclusion is acceptable (Claim) because it is drawn from the testimony of experts: psychiatrists, physicians, etc (Data). (p. 85).

Few modern textbooks on argumentation fail to cover the Toulmin model. You will find the Toulmin model helpful to apply in formal and in informal argumentation because its concepts are inherent in our commercial and legal as well as cultural and societal milieu. Borrowing from Toulmin, we will apply context-dependent (or context-variant) and context-independent (or context-invariant) argumentative discourse in this way. An arguer and argument are context-variant when they are highly restricted to a particular set of circumstances to function or to function optimally. An arguer and argument are context-invariant when they do are not restricted to a particular set of circumstances to function or to function optimally (Toulmin, 1958).

Many arguers may be capable of presenting arguments that function superbly in a particular context, such as a law court or a scientific circle. They and their arguments may depend highly or wholly on their presentation in a court or a scientific colloquium; the arguers may be dependent on and restricted to a particular context of argumentative influence and power. The arguers may not be very successful in arguing without their familiar contexts; they may be restricted to specified contexts for success. When this condition applies, the arguers are context-dependent. However, some arguers may be capable of presenting arguments that function superbly across contexts; they may not be restricted to specific contexts nor dependent on specific contexts alone for success. Instead of being persuasive only in court or in a scientific setting, some arguers may present arguments that are convincing in many contexts. When this condition applies, the arguers are context-invariant. We view context-invariant in a relative manner. Arguers who can argue effectively in numerous contexts would earn praise for being context-invariant; their power of argumentation transcends any one context. They are not restricted to but one arena of argumentation.

For example, an attorney may be highly skilled in the courtroom graces of argumentation yet be unable to function effectively at a town meeting; a politician may argue eloquently before an audience yet function minimally at home; and a scientist may argue convincingly to other scientists yet remain functionless outside the specialized judgment of other scientists. In short, we must learn to respect those skilled in argumentation in certain arenas yet remain objective about their potential effect and usefulness outside their special arena.

A worthy contribution to evaluating argumentation comes from the field of law itself. Kathleen Mahoney, a professor of law, introduces us to invaluable legal concepts in a manner that any of us can understand and apply. She covers rules and principles that are fundamental to law as we experience it in North American society. Her discussion presents guidelines for determining whether evidence may be judged relevant and admissible in a court. She also covers public and private writings that may be used as sources of evidence. Of course, the reliability and unreliability of the testimony of witnesses as evidence is explained. Mahoney also details the probative value of evidence: that is, its fact-finding function as in probing for the facts. She elaborates on presumption and burden of proof as they are used in legal contexts. And, she sketches two legal standards: the standard of *reasonable doubt* that is used as the criterion for judgment in cases prosecuted in criminal action and the standard of the *balance of probabilities* or the *preponderance of evidence* that is used as the criterion for judgment in cases prosecuted in a civil action. Of course, the standard of a preponderance of evidence is much lower in a civil action case than the standard of a reasonable doubt found in criminal cases. Please read Mahoney on pages 133-145.

With respect to legal evidence, several additional comments might prove helpful. Using *Blond's Evidence* (1994) as a source, the term *burden of proof* is an ambiguous term encompassing

72

two separate ideas: the burden of producing evidence and the burden of persuasion. The burden of producing evidence entails challenge, opportunity, and responsibility of going forward with evidence. The burden of persuasion involves "persuading the trier of fact that the fact at issue is true." To satisfy the burden of proof (or of producing evidence), a "party must produce some form of affirmative evidence, either direct or circumstantial." Evidence based on the "lack of credibility of opposing witnesses" does not satisfy the burden of proof (pp. 99-101).

To satisfy the burden of persuasion, the standard depends, and therefore differs, on a trial being civil or criminal. While the civil trial standard is "by a preponderance of evidence," the criminal trial standard is "beyond a reasonable doubt." An intermediate standard between these two extremes involves a standard "by clear and convincing evidence." The policy decisions behind these standards reflect the recognized societal consequences of the decisions to be reached through the trial. An erroneous outcome for a civil trial is seen as no worse for the plaintiff as for the defendant. An erroneous outcome for a criminal trial has more serious consequences. As a society, we have determined that it is preferable for a guilty person to go free than for an innocent person to be wrongly punished. Because the "stakes are higher, so is the standard of proof" (pp. 102-103).

The proof required calls for different levels of evidence. The type and amount of evidence varies. *Direct evidence* refers to "evidence which, if true, directly proves the fact at issue. Direct evidence that scientific fact contradicts does not satisfy the burden of producing evidence. *Circumstantial evidence* points to evidence of "other facts from which the trier of fact can infer the existence of the fact at issue, or which create a legal presumption of the fact at issue": the most fundamental definition of "presumption" being the "procedural rule or process by which the existence of fact B may be presumed by proof of the existence of fact A." *Quantity of evidence* entails the introduction of "sufficient evidence from which it would be possible, if viewed in the light most favorable to that party, to conclude the existence of the fact at issue." What constitutes sufficient evidence varies from fact to fact. And, the *quality of evidence* differs between jurisdictions and types of trials (pp.101-103).

Before ending this lesson, what must be mentioned about arguing is paying attention to consequences, material and formal. In analyzing and evaluating the value of our position or that of another, we might look to actual or perceived consequences. As symbol using creatures, we can both observe what follows from one action over another action and speculate on what may likely follow from one action over another. By observing or projecting the consequences, we can decide which path may be of benefit and which may not. So, for example, to take a clear example, we can look at hatha yoga and weight-training as modes of exercise. If we want to build sizable muscle over the next three months with minimal concern for risk of injury, we would be wise to embark on a weight-training program over a hatha yoga program since weight-training would have a higher probability of building sizable muscle in a short time. However, if we were interested in building muscle gradually with extremely low risk of injury over the next year, we would be wise to embark on a hatha yoga program over a weight-training program. The consequences of one program over the other can guide is in arguing for or against one or the other.

To draw an illustration from the world of business, policies and profits can be analyzed and judged by consequences too. For instance, UnoCo, a hypothetical company, has a policy of setting prices locally to get an edge on the competition in any particular area. CincoCo, another hypothetical company, has a policy of setting prices locally only after obtaining permission from its central office. UnoCo finds Tide selling for $5.50 at CincoCo and has the authority to lower its price on this item immediately, so UnoCo lowers its price to $5.00 instantly. CincoCo learns of this but has to await approval from its main office. This takes 10 working days. In the meantime, UnoCo sells 10,000 units of this product while CincoCo sells but 1,000 units of this product. The consequences of the UnoCo policy results in a competitive advantage in sales whereas the consequences of the CincoCo policy results in no such sales advantage. By scrutinizing consequences, we can analyze and even determine whether to side one way or another.

REFLECTIONS: Agreements, Conflicts, and Questions

To seek and find fallacies, do you have to be a logician? Is it not true that argumentative analysis is a logically demanding power that only logicians should exercise? How can everyday people logically examine complex discourse to determine whether an argument has been made with or without fallacies? How can any of us separate formal from informal fallacies? Is this not a specialized task for logicians and philosophers only? Critical thinking is so demanding. How can any of us come to grips with critical thinking? Is it not safer, easier, and wiser to discuss fallacies in general than to analyze fallacies into formal and informal? Is it not safer, easier, and wiser to discuss informal fallacies in general rather than discuss fallacies of ambiguity, presumption, and relevance? Only philosophers and academic would have any use for such hair-splitting distinctions anyway, correct?

LESSON FOUR

Managing Conflict: Inviting and Avoiding

Lesson Objectives:

To provide an overview of managing conflict

To discuss conflict resolution and argumentation

To apply the roles of devil's and angel's advocate

To explain argumentation success levels (or circles) for analyzing conflict

To introduce risk assessment

Managing Conflict

Conflict management deals with controlling disagreements, fights, tensions, clashes, and other controversial encounters between human beings. In argumentation, conflict management pertains to how we choose to handle conflicting, contradictory, and hostile communication reasonably. As a reminder, our notion of argumentation in this course is broad. While it includes the tactics of a debate, argumentation as discussed in this course includes human conflict in general and its potential management. Managing interpersonal conflict entails resolving, and sometimes escalating, a fray. By analogy, anyone interested in competitive sports can learn much from a wrestling or soccer coach; however, that same person can learn much from a broad system of public control like police peace-keeping. Argumentation as used here addresses the winning tactics, let us say, of the wrestling coach along with the winning strategies of the police peace-keeper. If we consider the harmonizing and cooperative features of argumentation over its competitive ones, the argumentation in this course utilizes dance training in the waltz or the tango but also guidance in movement education or balancing team acts.

To ensure that argumentation serves to enhance democratic principles of open and free discussion from multiple points of view and to ensure that dissenting views are expressed with conviction and thoroughness, we suggest an ancient practice with two sides possible: the role of the *devil's advocate* and the role of the *angel's advocate*. These roles can be used to prevent groupthink disasters as well as ensure diverse opinions and reasons are expressed. An advocate is anyone who advances an idea to others. The devil's advocate would be someone who tries to say everything a devil would say against someone or something before enthronement is offered; the angel's advocate would be someone who tries to say everything an angel would say in favor of someone or something before dethronement is offered. So, when a person or idea is set forth to be praised in some way, a devil's advocate speaks against it to increase the chance that its acceptance has been sufficiently attacked; and, when a person or idea is set forth to be condemned, an angel's advocate speaks for it to increase the chance that its rejection has been sufficiently attacked.

Both roles attempt to guarantee that opposite and dissenting views are presented and respected for the benefit of all involved in the making decisions. Both roles attempt to attack what an individual or group judgment that may be made without reasonable criticism. Neither role may provide alternative plans. While both attack an idea or ideal being presented, neither has to provide an alternative plan. The role of *creative advocate* can be used for this purpose. The creative advocate is someone who sees and promotes options not considered or creates options where none exist. The motto of this advocate is: *Aut viam inveniam aut faciam* (I will either find a way or make one). The creative advocate is an open-ended or free-wheeling advocate. The creative advocate need not go with the person (or idea) opposed by the devil's advocate nor the person (or idea) supported by the angel's advocate. Their way is the way that has not yet been found or formed but needs to be. Borrowing from O'Hair, Friedrich, and Dixon (2002, p. 322), a pharmaceutical company deliberating on a new hypertension drug in the form of a pill may have proponents who endorse it despite its side-effects of growing hair in undesirable areas and opponents who want to stop making it. A third group of creative advocates may suggest that the drug be put in the form of an ointment and applied topically to areas that grow hair only where desired.

We provide a general account of conflict management (Fiordo, 1990, pp. 41-44) on interpersonal conflict escalation and resolution that stems from the text by Joyce Hocker and William Wilmot (2002) as well as sources that are ancient and modern, Eastern and Western, global and local. Inarguably, not all conflict and argumentation should be engaged nor avoided. Some conflict and argumentation should be sought and some avoided. Not all conflict and argumentation is productive nor does it advance relations and the pursuit of truth. Some conflict and argumentation is unproductive and even counterproductive; some is useful and beneficial. Each situation has to be assessed before engaging others in conflict or avoiding clash. To clash may have class or it may not. To welcome conflict does not necessitate inviting disaster. Though arguing need not serve as a synonym for quarrelling or fighting. We can argue with mutually beneficial results. Besides, if innovation or improvement in a standard or practice is called for, conflict may be inevitable (Fiordo, 1990, p. 41).

The article by Steven C. Combs entitled "Sun-zi and the *Art of War*: The Rhetoric of Parsimony" cited in the references is valuable for assessing the management of conflict. A second contributor to the topic of conflict management included here is Stephen Littlejohn. He covers conflict resolution with reasonable care. He discusses the Prisoner's Dilemma. You will find this game of conflict, strategy, and consequences fascinating and helpful. And, he expands on the notion of dialectic theory in human relationships. We will sketch here the way Littlejohn (2002) explains attribution theory and its tie to conflict. Attribution theory addresses the "ways people infer the causes of behavior." Attribution theory predicts that we develop our own theories to explain the conflicts in which we are involved, and these theories are predominantly a part of our attributions. So, how we deal with a conflict depends on how we place blame. We create conflicts, in short, on how we assign blame (p. 257). To counteract this tendency to have conflict over our attributions of blame, Littlejohn presents a perspective from the work of Alan Sillars. Sillars suggests three strategies for dealing with conflict in interpersonal relations: strategies that avoid or minimize conflict, strategies designed to win a conflict, and strategies that strive to achieve outcomes that are positive and reciprocal for both parties to a conflict. With respect to the integrated relation of attribution and conflict management, Sillars argues that attributions significantly determine the definition and outcomes of conflicts in at least three ways: 1) the attribution of individuals in conflict determine which strategies they will choose to manage the conflict; 2) biases in the process of attribution "discourage the use of integrative strategies"; and, 3) the strategy selected influences the outcome of the conflict. Hence, cooperative strategies favor integrative solutions and information exchange in communicative conflicts while competitive strategies may escalate conflict and lead to unsatisfactory solutions (pp. 257 & 259).

One more perspective on conflict comes to us from Robert Heath and Jennings Bryant (2000, pp. 241-257). Their comments on the role of power and limits of deceit in human communication and conflict are extremely useful. We manage conflict so differently. Conflict management stresses the relational component over the content component of argumentation and will give you additional information on the consequences of dealing with issues: the sensitive matter of confronting issues others through non-confrontational as well as confrontational means. Heath and Bryant tell us that we expect to communicate with one another in certain ways. We expect certain communication styles, strategies, and messages to be used at different times in a relationship. When our interpersonal communication expectations are met, the "relationship is rewarding" (p. 241).

When our interpersonal communication expectations are not met, our expectations are violated and conflict may result. When conflict surfaces, we have a choice. We may choose to respond from a wide list of options that range from confrontation to avoidance. We form our personalities and selves through "actions with others" (p.250). Once we have contact and formed a relationship with another, the relationship must "sustain periods of conflict." To maintain a relationship or have it grow, its rewards must outweigh its costs. Otherwise, the relationship will likely dissolve. Building relationships involves a "dialectic of moving from autonomy to interdependence." When we communicate interpersonally and subsequently build, maintain, and dissolve relationships, we are involved in "dialectical processes" (pp.250-251). Handling conflict involves dialectics. Conflict, however, need not be mere misunderstanding; nor is it "necessarily resolved by clarity." Since people "in conflict may understand one another quite clearly," not clarity, but incompatibility, may cause conflict. Moreover, conflict need not be "inherently harmful to relationships"; rather, conflict can even strengthen relationships (pp. 252-253). When conflict resolution, however, becomes our objective, a number of strategies are available to increase, reduce, and manage conflict. To resolve interpersonal conflict, as communicators and arguers, we have available to us "collaborative decision making, compromise, competition, accommodation, and avoidance" (p. 253). In a conflict, because one person has the ability to influence another, one factor that is central to accomplishing this end is power. Power, of course, is "enacted through moves and countermoves." In short, how we "approach conflict is vital to whether it is likely to be resolved" (p. 254).

Success Levels (or Circles)

You are asked to think about conflict management in the broad context of stimuli: human behaviors, arguments, conflicts, and fallacies. The following classifications, called here *argumentation success levels (or circles)*, should guide you in analyzing and assessing conflict. Based on the psychology of perception and selective attention, they should help you to define the material and psychological space around you at any given time. Success is the defined goal at the diverse levels toward which you should strive or consider striving. To manage conflict, please reflect on the following four *levels* of the four basic dynamics. Four key features of stimuli are presented below: behavior, argument, conflict, and fallacies. Although more than these four can be diagramed as success levels (circles), the four below are presented for didactic purposes to guide you toward a more effective way of analyzing and managing behavior in diverse situations:

STIMULI

A. Behavior

All that is happening in a situation

_____

What we are aware of

_____

What we respond to

_____

What we respond to successfully

B. Argument

All arguments in a situation

_____

Arguments we are aware of

_____

What arguments we respond to

_____

Arguments we respond to successfully

C. Conflict

All conflicts in a situation

_____

Conflicts we are aware of

_____

Conflicts we respond to

_____

Conflicts we respond to successfully

D. Fallacy

All fallacies in a situation

_____

Fallacies we are aware of

_____

Fallacies we respond to

Fallacies we respond to successfully

In a situation involving argumentation, we might use these levels to analyze and assess our communicative actions and their success. We can assume that stimuli in general as well as behaviors, arguments, conflicts, and fallacies occur in any situation. We might create or construct factors as well. In short, some stimuli may be noticed in the sense that we create them or define them. This human activity may derive from our symbolic processing and our capacity to use abstract language. So, we perceive what is present through our linguistic and cultural filters. In any situation, there are behaviors, arguments, conflicts, and fallacies of which we are aware; that is, we select, notice, highlight, emphasize, abstract, or perceive some stimuli. Also, there are stimuli of which we are not aware; that is, behaviors, arguments, conflicts, and fallacies we recognize and fail to recognize. Furthermore, there are going to be stimuli we respond to unsuccessfully and successfully. In fact, we may respond to none of these factors successfully.

We may plot ratios with practical benefit especially from two (or more) levels: for example, those dealing with what we have become aware of and those we responded to successfully. Furthermore, we might have noticed (become aware of) 20 conflicts but handled (responded to) 10 successfully. This would give us a 2 to1 ratio for conflicts we noticed versus conflicts we managed with success. We might have observed 10 conflicts but handled 2 successfully. This would give us a 5 to 1 ratio for conflicts we noted versus conflicts we treated successfully. Potentially, additional features from the first level of what is actually going on may surface upon reexamination. This situation can occur, for instance, when we videotape a verbal exchange or altercation. What was not seen in the primary experience may be recognized on the second or third reviews. We might remain open for our own advantage to a situation where we missed the stimuli on the direct experience but caught it on subsequent experiences. Thus, we might plot a ratio between all that is happening in a situation on first perception versus a second perception. On the first experience we might have been aware of 10 conflicts, but upon review we become aware of 20 conflicts. If we now confirm 20 conflicts and only 2 treated successfully, the ratio falls from 5 to 1 to 10 to 1. We know we have to improve our argumentation score. Since this ratio plotting tool can be employed with utility, please test it.

Two other practical means will be offered to help you manage conflict: strategizing on argumentative acts and on varying the media of argumentation. Although argumentative acts can be classified in a number of ways, we will call attention to two basic ones that should be easily identifiable. When faced with argumentation, a number of alternative strategies can be considered. We will look at the following options for dealing with the expression of disagreement:

1. Engagement: direct or indirect, limited or total, assertive or aggressive actions
2. Non-engagement: absence of engagement
    a. Avoidance: no argumentative action at all
    b. Evasion: deliberation on a limited basis with engagement circumvented or diffused
    c. Postponement: avoidance for now but possible, or likely, engagement later
    d. Defense: deliberation that inquires about or counters assertions but lacks advocacy of a
        positive plan
    e. Refusal: stonewalling parties pressuring participation in conflict and argumentation
    f. Disengagement: withdrawal from engagement

The preceding strategic items do not exhaust the possibilities. The categories are constructs, not absolutes. Other strategic categories might classify the argumentative acts with other purposes in mind. We offer these as guidelines only. For practical purposes, you may decide between two basic options under the circumstances and in light of the parties involved: namely, *engagement* or *non-engagement* or *to engage* or *not to engage*.

When faced with argumentation, varying the <u>contexts</u> (locations and situations) and <u>channels</u> of communication (media) may serve to manage conflict efficiently also. Contexts may be selected based on how public or private they may be, how formal or informal they may be, early or late in the day, before or after certain events, and other situational factors considered to be germane to the decision to engage another or not in argumentation. Communication media vary significantly in 2011 and into the foreseeable future, and their numbers are growing with each advancing telecommunication invention.

Special attention will now go to communication media that might employed to bring about successful effects in argumentation. With no attempt to exhaust the multitudinous channels, the following selection of media potpourri is offered. While the following media options are frequently used, they are seldom systematically alternated and combined. However, for optimal, strategic argumentative effect, it would be wise to consider mixing and varying them.

1. Face-to-face: a multi-modal channel requiring complex and strong control over self, others, and circumstances

2. Telephone: an auditory channel requiring limited control over self, others, and circumstances

3. Audio recording sources (e.g., CDs and tapes): an auditory channel requiring limited control over self and perhaps others

4. Email: a visual and auditory channel requiring limited control over self and perhaps others

5. Conventional mail: a usually visual channel requiring limited control over self and others

6. Emerging media technologies (Dumova & Fiordo, 2010a & 2010b): social interaction technologies and collaboration software, blogs, twitters, web sites, cell phones, CDs, videos, and other indirect and mediated channels for conducting argumentation (e.g., iPhones and iPads)

7. Mass media: the complexity of the Internet, newspapers, radio, and television (e.g., letters to the editor and TV interviews).

8. Interlocutors: messengers, friends, go-betweens, representatives, public relations specialists, attorneys, mediators, arbitrators.

9. Artifact sources: currency, candy, jewels, clothing, foods, drinks, cars, and other things that can be used as symbolic carriers of meaning (e.g., in American commercials, consumers are urged to say it with – diamonds, gold necklaces, chocolate, cologne, etc.)

10. Nonverbal signals: channels of touch, smell, sight, taste, and hearing used as symbolic carriers of meaning (e.g., communicators might say "I'm sorry" with a hug, a kiss, or an embrace).

The preceding strategic items can be utilized in the following practical ways with various parties under diverse conditions. When a complex case is being made to someone of superior rank, an arguer might decide, based on unique circumstances and personalities, to initiate the argumentation via a letter. Follow up contributions to the letter may involve email, telephone, and eventually a face-to-face presentation. When face-to-face, the arguer may choose not to speak but only to look at the other and hold that person's hand. Another set of circumstances and personalities involving argumentation might call for an arguer to initiate argumentation through a go-between, such as a friend or colleague, and advance it with a face-to-face interview followed by email, telephone messages, and a ticket to a Broadway production. Clearly, an arguer may initiate and advance argumentation in one medium and go to no other medium. However, practical circumstances may allow the deliberation to proceed more readily through multiple channels of communication rather than through just one. In fact, an arguer may proceed like a campaigner moving from one medium to several other media.

Before leaving this discussion of managing conflict, several practical tips on handling small conflicts that can grow into major conflicts will be offered. The conflict reducing techniques are ways to resolve needless and mindless conflict. One strategy is to check things out by reference to experience through the senses or through official recorded sources; the procedure of verifiability through the sense (and their scientific extensions) for dealing with willful and egocentric conflicts is corrective and preventive. General semanticists call this an "extensional orientation." If someone argues that it is a "cold day," rather than argue over words, you might step outside for yourself to see whether your subjective use of the word "cold" is shared or whether you might use the word "cool" to describe the day. You might also ask the person declaring it to be a "cold day" to translate the subjective word "cold" into an intersubjective (or objective) common standard that can be mutually verified, such as "–15 centigrade but –40 centigrade with wind chill factored in." Another case would be this. Rather than quarrel endlessly about how many towns have the name *Eureka*, you might agree to an authoritative source, such as a current edition of the *National Geographic Atlas of the World,* and discover that 11 towns have that name and that four other places have the name *Eureka* as part of their name – for example, *Eureka Sound* in Canada.

Risk Communication

        Risk communication entails assessment rooted in analysis. Risk analysis is a relatively new and inexact science (DiSanza & Legge, 2003, pp. 267-268). Renz (1992) tells us that since democracy is based on "helping people make informed choices," risk communication devotes itself to "putting technology in service of democracy" (p. 9). Risk science aims to measure quantitatively "the risk posed by a particular hazard or measure the costs or benefits of a specific risk" (DiSanza & Legge, p. 267). Many risk studies map the relationship between exposure to a hazard and its consequences. Some risk studies analyze risks across large populations and "examine the costs of reducing a risk." No matter how much it attempts to yield "certainty in results, risk analysis is always subject to a variety of constraints that make the conclusion less than definitive" (pp. 267-268).

        Furthermore, risk analysis has limitations and is inexact. There are many "sources of imperfect knowledge" in risk analysis. For example, estimating the probable harm of a substance given to humans can be difficult. Subsequently, the "limitations of risk analysis pose an ethical dilemma for risk communicators." A risk communicator may have to decide whether to "focus on the bottom-line conclusions of a risk study and omit a necessarily complicated discussion of limitations." Ultimately, regardless of the accuracy of the scientific study, as a scientific study, a study in risk analysis cannot address value and policy questions. Yet, risk analysis is a helpful first step in the process of risk communication (p. 268).

Risk communicators must also examine their audience's perception of risk – factors leading to different degrees of concern about hazards. As an audience, for instance, we will have more concern about a hazard if we perceive the hazard to be involuntary, unnatural, memorable, dreaded, and unfair. We will also have more concern about a hazard if we perceive we have no control over it and are not familiar with it. As an audience, we will have less concern about a hazard if we perceive the hazard to be voluntary, within our control, natural, familiar to us, not memorable to us, not dreaded by us, and fair (pp. 270-271). As a risk communicator, you may have to work from the point of view of risk scientists who "believe the elimination of risk is an impossible goal." Consequently, risk analysis may be discussed in the form of tradeoffs in which the "risks and benefits of various hazards are compared and contrasted." So, we might tradeoff the comparative hazards of nuclear power with coal-fired plants or the purchase of a large car over a small car. To help us decide on which risk to take, we might employ risk comparisons that will "put various risks into perspective." For example, the comparative risk of dying in a motor vehicle accident is 1 in 4,000 while in an airplane it is 1 in 100,000 (pp. 280-281).

Risk communicators are not likely to encourage us to avoid all activity to reduce risk since "risk can never be totally eliminated from any situation" and since "nothing is completely safe" (Laudan, 1994, p. 8). The goal then is "not one of avoiding risks altogether but rather one of managing risks in a sensible way." And, risk management entails common sense and knowledge about the nature and "magnitude of the risks we many be running." We should aim to prepare ourselves for probable risks and take precautions against the more probable ones. We need to know not only what is risky but the magnitude or level of risk involved. Hence, if the likelihood of ingesting a toxin in a canned good is 1 in 10 million, we might eat the item without much concern. However, if the likelihood were 1 in 100, we might not eat the item. Taking the risk, though, depends on whether we are high, moderate, or low risk takers. A high risk taker might eat the canned good and risk the toxin even if the risk is 1 in 100; a moderate risk taker might eat the item and take a risk of 1 in 1,000; and, a low risk taker – someone who wants to minimize risk – may eat the item only if the risk is 1 in 10 million (pp. 8-13).

Of course, individual perception on risk varies tremendously, and there are misconceptions about risk. A gap can be predicted between our estimate of the magnitude of a risk and its actual threat. As an illustration, an American might believe the odds of dying in a car accident this year to be 1 in 70,000 whereas it is closer to 1 in 7,000. In addition, we tend to "minimize or underestimate the size of common risks" and "exaggerate the size of rare or unusual ones." Risk scientists might look for "divergences between perceived risks and real ones" and caution us that death by botulism is not several thousand times more common than we might think it is. Furthermore, having accurate estimates of the magnitude of comparative risk is not merely academic. What we decide to do depends partly on how risky we judge a situation to be. If we "misjudge the size of a risk by as much as 1,000 percent – and that is the usual level of error between the normal person's perception of a risk and its true value – then most of us are, most of the time, making ill-informed decisions." When we underestimate common risk and exaggerate rare ones, we foolishly protect ourselves against the unlikely dangers while failing to protect ourselves against the dangers most likely to hurt us (pp. 13-15).

Another way to consider managing risk is to see it as involving two strategies: prevention and mitigation. *Prevention* refers to lowering the "probability of an unwanted event" while *mitigation* refers to rendering the "consequences less unpleasant when [the unwanted event] does happen." As regards disease, prevention becomes prophylaxis while mitigation becomes therapeutics. Most of the time, *prevention* will "mean only to lower the probability" since total prevention may not be possible (Lewis, 1990, p. 69). One valuable tool for risk management is cost-benefit analysis. We might analyze the costs and benefits of, for example, a technology such as cell phones and compare life with cell phones to life without them (p. 97). Risk management might also include the analysis of causal relationships. When analyzing risk, it may be difficult to assign cause since there are "usually several contributing causes" in complex affairs and consequently it may not be "possible to establish which was *the* cause." In effect, it may only be possible to assign a probable cause for an event and not the cause for an event, for there is uncertainty of cause in two directions. In other words, a "cause may not have a unique effect, and an effect may not have a unique cause." The uncertainty is intrinsic to the effort to work things out (p. 101). In analyzing risk, faulty conclusion must be avoided. More often than not, risk analysis is "dominated by those who have easily understood solutions, easy-to-hate villains, and painless cures" (p. 174). Referring again to the Mencken Rule, H.L. Mencken quips: "There's always an easy solution to every human problem – neat, plausible, and wrong" (p. 48). We must exercise sound judgment to proceed with intelligence when those around us are seeking quick and easy answers to complex problems.

This section on risk communication will end with a version of a risk assessment matrix the US Army (2006) provides. It entails an assessment of risk that takes the severity of the hazard and the probability of the hazard occurring into account. The risk probability for a hazard ranges from frequent to unlikely while its severity ranges from catastrophic to negligible. Although the US Army uses five categories of probability and four categories of severity in the matrix, we will use but three and three. You may use what the US Army suggests or have more categories in your matrix. The risk level will be signified by E (extremely high), H (high), M (moderate), and L (low). The risk level includes the overall assessment of implementing the task in light of the hazards with countermeasures implemented. *Catastrophic* means major damage; *middling* means significant to minor damage; and, *negligible* means little or no damage. *High probability* means the likelihood of the event occurring is frequent (perhaps, a chance of 95 percent or more); *medium probability* means the likelihood of the event occurring is occasional (perhaps a chance of 40 to 60 percent); *low probability* means the likelihood of the event occurring is seldom or unlikely (perhaps a chance of five percent or less). Our matrix follows:

RISK ASSESSMENT MATRIX

	Probability		
Severity	High	Medium	Low
Catastrophic	E	H	M
Middling	E-H	H-M	L
Negligible	M	L	L

To apply this matrix to personal and social concerns would demonstrate its utility. For example, the risk of nuclear contamination from the meltdown of a nuclear power plant might be judged as M overall if we determine it would be rare but catastrophic. If we have grounds to believe the nuclear power plant was built in a hasty and careless manner without adequate safety measures, we might evaluate the risk overall as E since the severity would be catastrophic and the probability of it occurring high. You might do likewise with the risk to health of steroid abuse or the risk to world safety of Iran developing nuclear weapons. Of course, note that the estimates of risk may vary sizably.

In conclusion, assessing risk includes taking into account probability and consequences. One category deserving emphasis is low probability risks with catastrophic consequences that must be taken seriously, such as a large earthquake (Lewis, 1990, pp. 50 & 14).

Dialectical Therapy and Relational Theory

Contributions to conflict management in argumentation can be found in dialectical therapy. Only a sketch will be provided here. You are urged to pursue this topic in depth on your own. Our interest focuses on the use of symbolic interaction in the form of argument intended to help oneself and others. The use of questions and probes with responses and answers can be expected. Please recognize that we believe you can borrow from these psychotherapies and benefit in your relationships. We are not suggesting that the method can be applied safely and effectively with psychologically disordered people by someone who is not a certified psychologist. In brief, be careful how you use these methods and ideas. The psychologist Marsha Linehan (1993) developed *dialectical behavioral therapy* or DBT. *Dialectical therapy* in this case refers to "systematically combining opposed ideas with the goal of reconciling them." The therapeutic strategy is to "alternate between accepting clients as they are and confronting their disturbing behavior to help them change." Therapists move between "acceptance and change within the context of a supportive therapeutic relationship." She emphasizes, in her dialectical therapy, new ways to analyze a problem and "develop healthier solutions, a process that stimulates change" (Halgin & Whitbourne, 2003, p. 346.

Another psychological contribution comes from the psychologist Albert Ellis (2000) and his *rational-emotive behavior therapy* or REBT. His argumentative approach to psychotherapy is based on the premise that "dysfunctional emotions are the product of dysfunctional thoughts." One aim of the REBT clinician entails cognitively restructuring a client. The clinician helps clients alter the way they view themselves, the world, and the future. The therapist "reframes negative ideas into more positive ones to encourage the development of more adaptive ways of coping with emotional difficulties." The therapist does this by questioning and challenging the "client's dysfunctional attitudes and irrational beliefs, and makes suggestions that the client can test in behavior outside the therapy session." In Ellis' REBT, the clinician tries systematically to "dissuade clients from their irrational beliefs by showing them how mistaken they are and helping them arrive at more rational ways of thinking about themselves." While Ellis can be "quite confrontational with clients," he contends that REBT is based on philosophical and humanistic psychology principles that "people can control their own destinies."

Furthermore, Ellis suggests that REBT can be applied with benefit in contexts outside of mainstream psychotherapy. He notes that REBT has been used effectively by religiously inclined therapists with philosophical views that include the acceptance of responsibility and a philosophy of non-perfectionism (Halgin & Whitbourne, 2003, pp. 131-132).

An illustration of dialectical forms of therapy might help you grasp how this unfolds. Clash is seen, of course, as potentially useful and necessary for making headway toward independence and health. Ellis and others can be seen on videotape demonstrating their therapeutic methods. You might check with your video library to see whether the video is available. In the meantime, this example might give you an idea. We will use an REBT hypothetical therapist. Consider this case. At 22 Pat is troubled over not being promoted at work and goes to Dr. REBT. Dr. REBT would try to uncover Pat's irrational beliefs that cause him/her to feel upset and frustrate any opportunity for success in the future. Dr. REBT would aim to show Pat that viewing a job alone as a source of self-worth is irrational and would suggest a more rational belief for Pat. The more rational belief might be presented to Pat in a sentence such as this for Pat to repeat: "It was disappointing for me not to get the promotion I so much wanted, but I have other rewards in life outside my work." Dr. REBT might also assist Pat in accepting that there will be future opportunities and that all is not lost for Pat unless there is self-sabotage at the current place of employment (p. 132).

In the video of Dr. Ellis in a therapy session with a client, in fact, he engages the client in a therapeutic debate to reeducate the client on irrational beliefs held and rational beliefs that should be held. Ellis uses scientific, factual, and verifiable grounds predominantly to establish rational beliefs. If we were to apply REBT to non-clinical situations where healthy people are confused, inaccurate, or misinformed, we might attack the irrational beliefs they hold as true. For example, raised in Dunseth, North Dakota, Jade has been offered a job upon graduation in Norway but does not want to take it because he thinks the country is too small for its population in comparison to countries he has visited and likes, such as Portugal and Italy. Being raised in rural North Dakota, Jade prefers a lot of land per person. A rational helper might ask him whether land area and population are serious factors in his decision. If Jade confirms that the size of the country and population are critical factors, then the rational helper might replace Jade's irrational beliefs with rational beliefs. The helper might make a case for Norway based on facts from a reputable current almanac (say 2006) and argue as follows. Norway has a land area of 118,865 square miles with a population density of 37 per square mile. In contrast, Portugal has a land area of 35,502 square miles with a population density of 296 per square mile while Italy has a land area of 113,522 square miles with a population density of 500 per square mile (Almanac, 2006). On the grounds Jade has declared, Norway would be a wise decision comparatively, for it has more land area and a far lower population density.

Relational Dialectics Theory

Lastly, contributions to conflict management in argumentation can be found in relational dialectics theory. Only a sketch will be provided here as well. You are urged to pursue this topic in depth on your own. For the most complete expression of this theory, we urge you to read *Relating: Dialogues and Dialectics* (1996) by Leslie Baxter and Barbara Montgomery. In this theory, "multiple points of view play off one another in every contradiction" (West & Turner, 2004, p. 206). In the words, of Baxter and Montgomery (1996), dialectical "thinking is not directed toward a search for the 'happy mediums' of compromise and balance, but instead focuses on the messier, less logical, and more inconsistent unfolding practices of the moment" (p. 46). In relational dialectics theory, "contradictions or tensions between opposites never go away and never cease to provide tension." They are a constant in relational life. A major communication task is to manage these tensions. Change and transformation are indicative of relational interaction, not homeostasis (West & Turner, 2004, p. 207).

In relational dialectics theory, three basic and interactive relationships are critical: autonomy and connection, openness and protection, and novelty and predictability. With autonomy and connection, we face conflicting tensions between being close and being separate. With openness and protection, we confront conflicting tensions between sharing our secrets and keeping them hidden. With novelty and predictability, we recognize conflicting tensions between the comfort of stability and the excitement of change. Interactive dialectics occur "within the relationship itself" and are a part of the "partner's interaction with each other." There are also contextual dialectics or "tensions resulting from the place of the relationship within the culture." With contextual dialectics, there are tensions that result from "private relationships and public life" as well as tensions that result from "the difference between idealized relationships and lived relationships" (pp. 209-213). While dialectic tensions between communicators are ongoing, efforts are made to manage the tensions (p. 214).

Is not managing conflict just another way of talking about people in power who use any means necessary, ethical or otherwise, to squelch differences? Is not conflict resolution is a cowardly way of avoiding real conflict? How could someone escalate a conflict as a way of reducing or resolving the conflict? Are these not incompatible goals? If we want to resolve conflict, should we not do everything in our power to keep it from escalating? Should we not avoid the conflict altogether if we can? How can we assess argumentation by analyzing consequences? Of what practical value are the argumentation success levels? Do the argumentation success levels even make sense? How could we benefit from using these levels? Why would we want to use them? And, of what value to argumentation are the methods of empirical science?

LESSON FIVE

Ethics in Inquiry, Advocacy, and Transformation

Lesson Objectives:

To discuss what argumentation and communication scholars consider ethical in dialog, debate, and discussion

To examine where ethics overlaps with legality

To explain the rational bias and standards of argumentation

To provide an overview of ethics

Overview

Theodore Roosevelt, the 26th US President, asserted that to educate a person "in mind, and not in morals, is to educate a menace to society." Although we agree with Roosevelt's sentiments and suggest an operational ethic, we do not prescribe an ethic of communication and argumentation for you. You will have to choose your own ethic. However, we will provide you with a practical notion of ethics that is suggested as a workable ethic in everyday North American life. Incidentally, the word *ethics* derives from the Greek word *ethos*. *Ethos* means "character." With respect to a general working definition of *ethics*, we will use the following: "moral principles for living and making decisions." Subsequently, we have to note that the word morality derives from the Latin word *moralis*. *Moralis* means "customs or manners." Nonetheless, we must be careful that insofar as we may obtain our ethics from the society surrounding us, we become vulnerable to the distortions and biases of the values our society teaches us and endorses (Leslie, 2000, pp. 16-17).

The National Communication Association (NCA) suggests ethical principles that can be useful for communicating in our diversified and pluralistic society. As West and Turner (2003) assert, our "ethics will always be challenged at work." They suggest we "stay focused on what is right and wrong at work." They urge us to be honest with ourselves. Since "ethics surrounds us each day," being an ethical person is the "most important characteristic of being human" (p. 522). Being ethical or failing to be ethical constitutes the grounds on which others will judge us in specific contexts and in life in general.

The ethical communication principles from NCA (www.natcom.org) are presented here as reasonable and practical. The principles follow:

1. advocate truthfulness, accuracy, honesty, and reason as essential to the integrity of communication.
2. endorse freedom of expression, diversity of perspective, and tolerance of dissent to achieve the informed and responsible decision making fundamental to a civil society.
3. strive to understand and respect other communicators before evaluating and responding to their messages.
4. promote access to communication resources and opportunities as necessary to fulfill human potential and contribute to the well-being of families, communities, and society.
5. promote communication climates of caring and mutual understanding that respect the unique needs and characteristics of individual communicators.
6. condemn communication that degrades individuals and humanity through distortion, intimidation, coercion, and violence and through the expression of intolerance and hatred.
7. are committed to the courageous expression of personal convictions in pursuit of fairness and justice.
8. advocate sharing information, opinions, and feelings when facing significant choices while also respecting privacy and confidentiality.
9. accept responsibility for the short- and long-term consequences of our own communication and expect the same of others.

Please note well that the first principle stresses that veracity is necessary for communication to have integrity. Without veracity, we invite anarchy and chaos into our communication and life. Please note that the last principle emphasizes that we must be jointly responsible for the consequences of communication. All the principles have importance. For argumentation, all of the principles apply. We underscore the value of these two in particular.

For a general account of ethics and ethics in communication, you can turn to the writings of Rob Anderson and Veronica Ross (pp. 300-317); they introduce ethics with a discussion of the "whether" question: that is, the need to ask whether to act in a certain way (p. 301). The authors go on to distinguish deontological, teleological, and egalitarian approaches to ethics. They then explain a selection of ethical theories tied directly to communication and argumentation: Aristotelian or virtue ethics, Taoist ethics, dialogic ethics, and the feminine ethic of caring.

Deception, Detection, and Revealment

Deception theory in communication studies pertains to the use of falsification, concealment, and equivocation in everyday settings that presume trust and honesty as the modus operandi (Buller & Burgoon, 1996; Burgoon et al, 1999; Fiordo, 1999; & Burgoon, 2005). Those who wish to control and dominate others by any means necessary can be benevolent dictators, bullies, sadists, or even loving parents. An antidote to deception is what will be called here "detection theory." Detection theory counters falsification, concealment, and equivocation with verification, truth, accuracy, revealment, revelation, expose, honesty, and evidence that deception is at work. Once we accept that, in a culture like that of North America, a truth bias exists, we can expect that deception has a place. Since most in this culture may operate on honesty most of the time, those who do not can then take advantage of the honest ones through lies, concealments, evasiveness, and other forms of deceptive behavior. Detecting deception counteracts deception. Uncovering deception may then proceed to revealing the deception to others, as in the classic American film entitled "Mr. Smith Goes to Washington." The counteraction to a truth bias is a suspicion bias. Suspicion as a bias serves as an antidote to the truth bias.

However, when we shift to a suspicion bias, we may still have a biased perception of those around us. When we communicate with a truth bias, we distort those who lie by treating too many as if they are honest when they are not. When we communicate with a suspicion bias, we distort those who tell the truth by treating too many as if they are lying when they are not (Burgoon, 2005). In light of the North American truth bias, a suspicion bias serves well to counteract perceptual error in human communication. The reverse would be true in a suspicion culture. The range of deception is tremendous. As Burke (1961, p. 307) puts it, "once a believer is brought to accept mysteries [that is, the secretive and unexplained], he will be better minded to take orders without question from those persons whom he considers authoritative." Mowrer (1967) urges us to assess critically our own idols, values, and ultimate terms. Once we do, we are better suited to accept these values with whatever limitations we see fit after a legitimate critical assessment of the forces at play. If lying has become a communicative norm for us, we might want to reassess our actions and likewise assess our action with respect to an veracity or honesty or truth bias.

Burgoon (2005) reviews our presumption of truth and its limitations: that is, the truth bias. Humans are generally inclined to believe one another, even when told the other is lying. Believing others is a sort of mental shortcut for forming judgments, yet mental shortcuts lean us toward incorrect decisions. We also have a visual bias: that is, seeing is believing. We believe what we see. We tend to see conspicuous and unusual behavior as deceptive, even when it is not. We rely on faulty cues and therefore make inaccurate judgments. The eye gaze, for instance, does not reliably indicate deceit. We suffer from a mismatch between what we believe to be reliable signs of deception and "what are actual correlates of deceit." Trained interviewers – that is, experts at detection versus lay people – can be equally inaccurate in judging deceit. Indeed, sometimes experts can be more inaccurate because "their training may induce a lie bias or chronic suspicion." Experts risk committing the Othello error: that is, judging the innocent truthtellers as liars or deceivers. In effect, experts may suffer from hallucinations that others are lying when they are not. Of course, we also have a vested social "interest in overlooking infractions of social rules, lest we face the discomfiture of confrontations and conflict and the possible unraveling of the social fabric." A cooperative principle reflects this tendency to discount suspicious or curious behavior. Politeness theory predicts "tolerance of misrepresentation, equivocation, and concealment for the sake of interpersonal harmony." Although receivers register suspicious behavior of others, the skills of deceivers as senders of false messages are usually greater than the skills of receivers for decoding the deceptive communication. We must work diligently to recognize the truth of deception: that deception is at work and must be noted and revealed (Burgoon, 2005, pp. 13-14). Deception is at work in everyday communication as well as in formal argumentation. Detection and revelation become the antidotes.

Moral and Ethical Systems

Since a social orientation is attributed to ethics, the extremes of moral relativism and moral legalism are noted with caution. In other words, we do not endorse the notion that "all ethical systems are equal and that we are free to choose our own regardless of how others might be affected." Nor do we endorse the notion that "whatever is legal is ethical…and whatever is illegal is unethical" (Leslie, 2000, p. 18). Ethical relativism and ethical legalism may be seen as default ethical philosophies in North America; that is, they may be philosophies embraced in the absence of some other system. Nonetheless, one must be aware of the limitations of the default philosophies. The limitations of moral and ethical relativism can be recognized in feminist opposition to female circumcision, a practice in

94

some countries, as being absolutely intolerable, not relatively acceptable. The limitations of moral and ethical legalism can be recognized in the American legality, at one time, of slavery. While slavery was legal, eventually it was denounced as immoral and unethical.

O. Hobart Mowrer (1972), the psychotherapist and learning theorist, advises that we examine our values as a way of living our lives on sound grounds. He thought we should periodically analyze and assess our values and confront straightaway any actual or emerging value crisis. One place to begin, according to Mowrer, would be with religious and political values. Along with Mowrer, I suggest this is a wise point of departure as well. I would add to religion and politics, professional values as found in codes of professional conduct for teachers, doctors, professors, lawyers, journalists, nurses, public relations agents, ministers, politicians, and so on (Fiordo, 1990).

An overview of ethical theories is provided for you to find or create your own ethical path in communication and argumentation. Implicit in argumentation as reasoned and reasonable discourse, of course, is a tendency toward valid reasoning, evidence, and proof; there is also a tendency toward respecting the rights and humanity of others. This means that validly reasoned discourse and reasonable treatment of others may have many intelligent and decent prescriptions that rule in (and rule out) certain types of thinking and communicating: for example, carefully providing legitimate evidence is ruled in while maliciously using fallacies is ruled out. Except under rare conditions (e.g., a known homicidal maniac asking for directions for the whereabouts of an intended victim or a soldier on a military mission involving the deceit of the enemy), truth and honesty would preferred and would be seen as ethical while falsehood and lies would be seen as undesirable and unethical.

To practice argumentation involves in most circumstances integrating socially acceptable ethical values that have their own biases: the reasonable inclinations of those who participate with civility in dialogue, discussion, debate, and other argumentative forms of communication. The goal of ethical argumentation is usually, at least in degree, is to be good, right, and true – and, for some, even beautiful. In short, while argumentation includes the study of reasoned and reasonable discourse as well as thoughtless, fallacious, and unreasonable discourse, ethical argumentation is tendentious toward validly reasoned and reasonable discourse. Ethical argumentation has the obligation to inform someone fully before acquiring consent and to inform someone fully before asking for a vote. To inform another partially embodies argumentation by default, default that may be understandable or even justifiable depending on circumstances.

To consider ethics with respect to inquiry, advocacy, and transformation is to see ethics as practiced in argumentation in its many manifestations – especially, dialog, debate, and discussion. The topic of ethics will be dealt with here by discussing it in relation to discussion and debate concerns first. Then it will be discussed in relation to communication and life. In short, we will advance from specific to general notions of ethics. Some of these sources constitute additional and optional reading. You might read Jensen on ethics in spoken debate (pp.19-35). Allied with Jensen's comments on ethics in debate will be those of Brilhart, Galanes, and Adams (2001) on expressing disagreement ethically, negotiating principled agreement, alternative ethical procedures, and ethical common ground dialogue rules in small groups (pp. 318-325).

Then examine Gerald Wilson's explanation of ethical responsibilities for small groups and their members (pp. 25-27). Conclude by reviewing Matlon on ethics in courtroom communication and DeVito on the legal morality of questions during interviews. Matlon (1988) discusses the communication ethics lawyers must consider in relation to their clients (pp.107-108). DeVito (2003) explains and illustrates the lawfulness of questions as classified through the federal government's Equal Employment Opportunity Commission. He covers unlawful (and in these cases unethical) information requests, BFOQ (Bona Fide Occupational Qualification) questions, and answering questions that are and are not BFOQ questions; in light of complex and practical concerns, DeVito advises us to answer BFOQ questions and provides several suggestions on how to do so (pp. 240-243).

In addition, DeVito (2003) comments on the lawfulness of questions asked during employment interviews. The Equal Employment Opportunity Commission of the federal government has determined that some job interview questions are unlawful. Of course, while general federal guidelines for unlawful questions apply in all 50 states, each state may have additional restrictions on unlawful questions. Broadly speaking, unlawful areas may include the following: "age, marital status, race, religion, nationality, citizenship, physical condition, and arrest and criminal records." For example, although it may be legal to ask job applicants whether they meet a legal age requirement for a job and can prove it, it may not be legal to ask for the exact age (p. 240). Questions that are pertinent to the employment may be asked. These questions are called BFOQ questions or bona fide occupational qualification questions. DeVito tells us the test is easy: "Is the information related to your ability to perform the job?" Hence, questions that in general may be illegal may be legal under specific conditions (p. 242). For instance, the level of vision for pilots of special types of aircraft may need to be of a certain rating by the standards of ophthalmology for a person to qualify for the job.

DeVito (2003) suggests that as job candidates we should answer BFOQ questions. As for unlawful questions, he argues that as job applicants we might answer a part of an unlawful question we do not object to yet omit information we do not wish to provide. As job applicants we must keep in mind that many employment interviews are used to "keep certain people out, whether it's people who are older or those of a particular marital status, affectional orientation, nationality, religion, and so on." If a tactful approach does not work in a job interview when we are confronted with illegal questions, questions that are not BFOQ questions, and we do not want to answer these questions, we might "counter by saying that such information is irrelevant to the interview and to the position you're seeking." However, DeVito advises that as job applicants we should be "courteous but firm." If an interviewer persists with unlawful questions after this more direct strategy is utilized, DeVito maintains that we might then "explain that these questions are unlawful and that [we are] not going to answer them" (Ibid). For an alternative account on BFOQ questions, Adler and Elmhorst (2002) provide an excellent account (pp. 217-220).

After reading these specific views of ethics as they apply to argumentation in conversation, groups, and debate, you are invited to investigate additional sources providing general accounts of ethics and reasoning. Explore the comments by Richard Paul and Linda Elder (2001) (pp.100-112 & 235-238) on universal intellectual standards, problems with egocentric thinking, and essential intellectual traits. Paul and Elder provide an ethic of reasoning: that is, reasoning should involve evaluative criteria to be sound and not fallacious. In short, thinking should have valuable guidelines that make it ethical. The thinking guidelines Paul and Elder provide exceed, yet include, the following standards: a) "All reasoning has a purpose"; b) "All reasoning is based on assumptions"; c) "All reasoning is done from some point of view"; d) "All reasoning is based on data, information, and evidence"; e) "All reasoning contains inferences or interpretations by which we draw conclusions and give meaning to data"; and f) "All reasoning leads somewhere or has implications and consequences" (pp.103-104). To emphasize the final point here, reasoning has consequences; through argumentation, we can analyze and assess the consequences of statements and proofs to determine their past, present, or future desirability.

Since sexual harassment is illegal but also unethical, one concise statement of it by DeVito (2003) will be mentioned. Citing two attorneys, Petrocelli and Repa, as his source on sexual harassment, DeVito explains what types of behavior constitutes sexual harassment, how to avoid conveying messages that might be seen as sexual harassment, and what to consider doing if you think you are being sexually harassed. Since *sexual harassment* is defined as "any unwelcome sexual advance or conduct on the job that creates an intimidating, hostile or offensive working environment," sexually harassing behavior might include the following: showing pornographic pictures, making remarks about anatomy, conduct to which a reasonable person would object, physical molestation, and behavior that you have informed others of that offends you and you want terminated (p. 213).

Mental Health, Culture, the Mindful Dialectic, and Ethics

Since mental pathology may play a role in reasoning and arguing, Paul and Elder (2001) identify egocentric tendencies in our thinking that may be unethical, unreasonable, and unhealthy (p. 235). Again, ethics related to argumentation will have a reasonable inclination or bias that is announced and endorsed except for rare circumstances. The natural and perhaps pathological egocentric tendencies these authors explain include the following: righteousness, hypocrisy, blindness, absurdity, immediacy, memory, myopia, and oversimplification.

Egocentric righteousness causes us to "feel superior in the light of our confidence that we possess the *Truth* when we do not." Egocentric hypocrisy causes us to "ignore flagrant inconsistencies": for example, between the "standards to which we hold ourselves and those to which we expect others to adhere." Egocentric blindness prevents us from noticing "facts and evidence that contradict our favored beliefs and values." Egocentric absurdity prevents us from recognizing "thinking that has 'absurd' consequences." Egocentric immediacy causes us to "overgeneralize immediate feelings and experiences" in such a way that "when one event in our life is highly favorable or unfavorable, all of life seems favorable or unfavorable to us." Egocentric memory causes us to "forget" information and evidence that fail to "support our thinking" and to "remember" information and evidence that support our thinking. Egocentric myopia causes us to think in an "absolutist way within an overly narrow point of view." And, egocentric oversimplification causes us to "ignore real and important complexities in the world in favor of simplistic notions when consideration of those complexities would require us to modify our beliefs or values" (pp. 235-236).

Consistent with the views of argumentation and critical thinking presented by Paul and Elder (2001) are the views of psychologists Carole Wade and Carol Tavris (1993, p. xv) on critical thinking. You may utilize their positive and negative approach to critical thinking when you apply critical thinking to the polemical views expressed in the following editorials and position statements. In brief, Wade and Tavris approach critical thinking as not simply being negative, skeptical, and debunking. Critical thinking also involves the ability to "generate ideas, see implications, be creative with explanations, and ask imaginative questions." Critical thinking to them includes being positive, breaking out of preconceived categories, and being open-minded – but not so open-minded that "your brains fall out" (Ibid).

Cultural awareness should be considered when rendering an ethical judgment in argumentative communication. The mindful dialectic approach, ideally, takes cultural factors into account always when reasoning and communicating on the ethics of communication. In this text, the overwhelming assumption has been with rhetoric and argumentation as used primarily in North America or Western culture. The North American mainstream has served as the basis for commentary and counsel on argumentation. An entire book can and should be written on arguing across cultures or in different cultures. Even in North American life, alternative or optional cultural perspectives are available and viable. While the mainstream of rhetorical and argumentative discourse and theory favors the Western tradition, other traditions are not rejected so much as unknown. We urge arguers using the mindful dialectic to take culture into account in order to proceed in a reasonable and relevant manner with North America's other cultures: for example, African, Asian, and Amerindian.

Recently, a dissertation has been completed that addresses Amerindian oratory. The author, Dr. Cheryl A. Long Feather (2007), entitled her dissertation "A Lakota/Nakota/Dakota Model of Oratory." In the dissertation, Long Feather, advances the teachings and practices of Aboriginal American rhetoric and oratory as an alternative to that of the mainstream. Just as she makes the case for contributions to rhetoric and oratory from Native American people being integrated into mainstream's use of discourse, she suggests that contributions can be incorporated by the Western tradition from Asian, African, and other peoples as well. She also encourages Native people to learn the mainstream Western tradition in oratory. All traditions should benefit rhetoric and oratory among North Americans, even if the Western tradition in rhetoric and oratory prevails as the primary mode of discourse.

Focusing on Lakota, Nakota, and Dakota discourse, Long Feather (2007) present graphic models of Western and Native ways of arranging information and relating to audiences. The linear and sequential forms from the Western tradition are contrasted with the circular and swirling modes of Aboriginal Americans. The Western tradition might, for example, typically present an introduction, body, and conclusion in the form of a vertical rectangle. Aboriginal thinking on the arrangement of a speech and presentation of an argument might resemble a medicine wheel, a spider web, or flower like a daisy where a central point is made but is not made in the linear sequential manner of the mainstream. What might appear to be rambling or wandering is actually the speaker leaving and returning in a circular manner around a central idea (pp. 93 and 96).

In short, there are many ways to present ideas. Rhetoricians and arguers worth their weight in words would gladly consider other modes of arranging and delivering speeches. Native oratory is mentioned here to inspire students of argumentation to examine alternate ways of forming and delivering speeches. Speakers and audiences may both benefit from culturally adapting the message to its end. The mindful dialectic will, subsequently, fulfill its complex purpose more fully when cultural differences are respected through practical application to argumentative discourse and circumstances.

REFLECTIONS: Agreements, Conflicts, and Questions

If we grant that ethics is vital to communication and argumentation, what might we do to decrease the number of occasions on which people ignore and even violate ethics when deliberating on some matter? Maybe, we expect argumentation to be always what it cannot be - namely, ethical, especially in a denominational sense. With personal and material interests involved in a conflict or debate, how can we ensure that ethical discourse prevails? Is not too much importance placed on ethics in argumentation and reasoning? When, if ever, do the law and ethics overlap? How can we distinguish between questions that are BFOQ and those that are not? Why should some types of questions be illegal? How are some types of questions ethical? Why is some argumentation unethical? What does sexual harassment have to do with the law and ethics? What do theories of ethics, such as deontological ethics and the feminine ethic of caring, have to do with argumentation? Why should someone who studies argumentation be concerned with broad theories of ethics?

References

Adler, R. B., & Elmhorst, J.M. (2002). *Communicating at work: Principles and practices for business and the professions*. Boston: McGraw Hill.

Anderson, R., & Ross, V. (2002). *Questions of communication: A practical introduction to theory*. Boston: Bedford/St. Martin's.

Baxter, L. A., & Montgomery, B. M. (1996). *Relating: Dialogues and dialectics*. NY: Guilford Press.

Becker, M., Bowman, C. G., and Torrey, M. (1994). *Feminist Jurisprudence: Taking Women Seriously – Cases and Materials*. St. Paul, MN: West Publishing.

Blond, N.C., et al. (1994). *Blond's evidence, 3rd ed*. NY: Sulzburger & Graham.

Brilhart, J.K., Galanes, G.J., & Adams, K. (2001). *Effective group discussion: Theory and practice*. Madison, WI: McGraw-Hill.

Buller, D. B., & Burgoon, J. K. (1996). Interpersonal deception theory. *Communication Theory*, 6, 203-242.

Burgoon, J. K., et al. (1999). The role of conversational involvement in deceptive interpersonal interactions. *Personality and Social Psychology Bulletin*, 25, 669-685.

Burgoon, J. K. (2005). *Truth, lies, and virtual worlds*. Boston: Pearson.

Burgoon, J.K., Berger, C.R., & Waldron, V. R. (2000). Mindfulness and interpersonal communication. *Journal of Social Issues*, 56, 105-127.

Burke, K. (1966). *Language as symbolic action: Essays on life, literature, and method*. Berkeley: University of California Press.

Combs, S. C. (2000). Sun-zi and the *Art of War*: The Rhetoric of Parsimony. *Quarterly Journal of Speech, 86, 276-294*.

Conrad, C., & Poole, M.S. (2002). *Strategic organizational communication in a global economy*, 5th ed. Orlando, FL: Harcourt.

DeVito, J. A. (2003). *Human communication: The basic course, 9th ed*. Boston: A.B. Longman.

DeVito, J. A.(1996). *Messages: Building interpersonal skills, 3rd ed*. NY: HarperCollinsCollegePublishers.

Dues, M. & Brown, M.(2001). *The practice of organizational communication*. Boston: McGraw-Hill Primis.

Dumova, T., & Fiordo, R. (2010). *Handbook of research on social interaction technologies and collaboration software: Concepts and trends. I.* Hershey, PA: IGI Global.

Dumova, T., & Fiordo, R. (2010). *Handbook of research on social interaction technologies and collaboration software: Concepts and trends. II.* Hershey, PA: IGI Global.

Eisenberg, A. M., & Ilardo, J. A. (1972). *Argument: An alternative to violence.* Englewood Cliffs, NJ: Prentice-Hall.

Eemeren, F.H. van, & Grootendorst, R. (1984). *Speech Acts in Argumentative Discussions: A theoretical model for the analysis of discussions directed towards solving conflicts of opinion.* Dordrecht-Holland: Foris.

Ellis, A. (2000). Can rational emotive behavioral therapy (REBT) be effectively used with people who have devout beliefs in God and religion? *Professional Psychology: Research and Practice*, 31, 29-33.

Engel, S.M. (2000). *With good reason: An introduction to informal fallacies, 6th ed.* Boston: Bedford/St. Martin's.

Fiordo, R. (1990). *Communication in education.* Calgary: Detselig.

Fiordo, R. (2010a). Contributions to general semantics from Charles Morris: An abstraction. Paper presented at the National Communication Association Annual Conference, San Francisco, CA.

Fiordo, R. (2010b). Extensional orientation, discipline, and hegemony. Paper presented at the Institute for General Semantics Annual Conference, New York, NY.

Fiordo, R. (1978). Kenneth Burke's Semiotic. *Semiotica* 23, 53-75.

Fiordo, R. (1999). The darkness behind the light: The consequences of communicating extreme deceit. *Medicine, Mind, and Adolescence*, 15, 37-46.

Forni, P.M. (2002). *Choosing civility: The twenty-five rules of considerate conduct.* NY: St. Martin's Griffin.

Foss, S.K., Foss, K.A., & Trapp, R. (2002). *Contemporary perspectives on rhetoric, 3rd ed.* Prospect Heights, IL: Waveland Press.

Foss, S. K., & Griffin, C. L. (1995). Beyond persuasion: A proposal for an invitational rhetoric, *Communication Monographs* 62, 2-18.

Freeley, A.J. (1986). *Argumentation and debate: Critical thinking for reasoned decision making, 6th ed.* Belmont, CA: Wadsworth.

Frankfort, H. G. (2005). *On bullshit*. Princeton: Princeton University Press.

Garfinkel, H. (1967). *Studies in ethnomethodology.* Englewood Cliffs, NJ: Prentice-Hall.

Gilligan, C. (1982). *In a different voice. Cambridge, MA: Harvard University Press.*

Gramsci, A. (1971). *Selections from the prison notebooks.* (Q. Hoare & G. Nowell-Smith, Eds. & Trans.) NY: International Universities Press.

Gutenberg, N. (2007). Speech communication and rhetoric: A German perspective, unpublished manuscript. University des Saarlandes, Germany.

Halgin, R.P., & Whitbourne, S.K. (2003). *Abnormal psychology: Clinical perspectives on psychological disorders.* Boston: McGraw-Hill.

Hayakawa, S. I., & Hayakawa, A.R. (1990). *Language in thought and action, 5th ed.* NY: Harcourt Brace Javanovich.

Heath, R. L., & Bryant, J. (2000). *Human communication theory and research: Concepts, contexts, and challenges, 2nd ed.* Mahwah, NJ: Lawrence Erlbaum.

Hocker, J.L., & Wilmot, W.W. (1985). *Interpersonal conflict, 2nd ed.* Dubuque, IA: William C. Brown.

Hollingsworth, P. J. (Ed.). (2003). *Unfettered expression: Freedom in American Intellectual Life.* Ann Harbor: University of Michigan Press.

Hoover, J. D. (2002). *Effective small group and team communication.* NY: Harcourt College Publishers.

Hopfe, L.M., & Woodward, M.R. (2001). *Religions of the world*, 8th ed. Upper Saddle River, NJ: Prentice Hall.

Hopkins, J. (Ed.). (1992). *The Dalai Lama: The meaning of life from a Buddhist perspective*. Boston: Wisdom Publications.

Inch, E.S.,& Warnick, B. (2002). *Critical thinking and communication: The use of reason in argument.* Toronto: Allyn and Bacon

Infante, D. A. (1988).*Arguing constructively.* Prospect Heights, IL: Waveland Press. Jensen, J.V.(1981). *Argumentation: Reasoning in communication.* NY: D.Van Nostrand.

Korzybski, A. (2000). *Science and sanity: An introduction to non-Aristotelian systems and general semantics*, 5th ed. Brooklyn, NY: Institute of General Semantics.

Kodish, S.P., & Kodish, B. I. (2001). *Drive yourself sane: Using the uncommon sense of general semantics*, rev. 2nd ed. Pasadena, CA: Extensional Publishing.

Langer, E.J. (1989). *Mindfulness.* Reading, MA: Addison-Wesley.

Lathem, E. C. (Ed.) (1969). *The poetry of Robert Frost.* New York: Holt, Rinehart and Winston.

Laudan, L. (1994). *The book of risks: Fascinating facts about the chances we take every day.* NY: John Wiley & Sons.

Lee, I. J. (1949). *The language of wisdom and folly: Background readings in semantics.* New York: Harper & Brothers.

Leslie, L.Z. (2000). *Mass communication ethics: Decision making in postmodern culture.* Boston: Houghton Mifflin.

Levinson, M. H. (2002). *Practical fairy tales for everyday living.* New York: iUniverse.

Levinson, M. H. (2002). *The drug problem: A new view using the general semantics approach.* Westport, CT: Praeger.

Lewis, H. W. (1990). *Technological risk.* NY: W.W. Norton.

Linehan, M.M. (1993). *Cognitive-behavioral treatment of borderline personality disorder.* NY: Guilford Press.

Littlejohn, S.W. (2002). *Theories of human communication, 7th ed.* Belmont, CA: Wadsworth/Thompson Learning.

Lockney, T. M. (1986). An open letter to the North Dakota attorney general concerning search and seizure law and the exclusionary rule. *North Dakota Law Review*, 62, 17-33.

Lockney, T.M.. (1996). Justice Beryl Levine: Taking her title seriously in North Dakota criminal cases. North Dakota Law Review. 72, 967-1010.

Long Feather, C. (2007). *A Lakota/Nakota/Dakota model of oratory.* Unpublished dissertation. University of North Dakota.

Lotringer, S. (Ed.). (1989). *Foucault live (Interviews, 1961-1984).* Trans. Lysa Hochroth and John Johnston. New York: Semiotext (e).

Lunsford, A.A., Ruszkiewicz, J.J., & Walters, K. (2004). *Everything's an argument: With readings*, 3rd ed. Boston: Bedford/St.Martin's.

Mahoney, K. (1990). "Evidence and advocacy for educators," in R. A. Fiordo (Ed.) *Communication in education,* 133-145. Calgary: Detselig.

Makau, J.M., & Marty, D.L. (2001). *Cooperative argumentation: A model for deliberative communities*. Long Grove, IL: Waveland Press.

Matlon, R.J. (1988). *Communication in the legal process*. Chicago: Holt, Rinehart & Winston.

Miller, K. (2003). *Organizational communication: Approaches and processes*, 3rd ed. Belmont, CA: Thompson.

Morris, C. (1970). *Signification and significance: A study of the relations of signs and values*. Cambridge, MA: The MIT Press.

Mowrer, O.H. (Ed.) (1967). Morality and mental health. Chicago: Rand McNally.

Noddings, N. (1984). *Caring: A feminine approach to ethics and moral education*. Berkeley: University of California Press.

Paul, R., & Elder, L. (1999). *The miniature guide to critical thinking: Concepts and tools*. Dillon Beach, CA: The Foundation for Critical Thinking.

Rakow, L. F. (Ed.) (1992). *Women making meaning: New feminist directions in* communication. NY: Routledge.

Rapoport, A. (1950). *Science and the goals of man*. NY: Harper & Brothers.

Renz, M.A. (1992). Communicating about environmental risk: An examination of a Minnesota county's communication on incineration. *Journal of Applied Communication Research*, 20, 9.

Rieke, R.D., & Sillars, M.O. (1975). *Argumentation and the decision making process*. NY: John Wiley & Sons.

Rosenberg, M. B. (2005). *Nonviolent communication: A language of life*. Encinitas, CA: Puddle Dancer Press.

Sawin, G. (Ed.). (1995). *Thinking and living skills: General semantics for critical thinking*. Concord, CA: International Society for General Semantics.

Shockley-Zalabak, P. (2002). *Fundamentals of organizational communication: Knowledge, sensitivity, skills, and values*, ft ed. Toronto: Allyn and Bacon.

Sprague, J., & Stuart, D. (2006). *The speaker's handbook*. Toronto: Thompson Nelson.

Sturgis, A. (1993). *The standard code of parliamentary procedure*, 3rd ed. NY: McGraw Hill.

The world almanac and book of facts. (2006). NY: World Almanac Books.

Toulmin, S. (1958). *The uses of argument*. Cambridge: Cambridge University Press.

US Army (1997). *Risk Management Worksheet and Risk Assessment Matrix*. CDTCMD
    Reg 385-10 and FM 101-5, 31 May 1997.

Vande Berg, L. R., Wenner, L.A., & Gronbeck, B.E. (2004). *Critical approaches to*
    television, 2nd ed. NY: Houghton Mifflin.

Wade, C., & Tavris, C. (1993). *Psychology, 3rd ed.* NY: HarperCollinsCollegePublishers.

Willard, C.A.(1989). *A theory of argumentation*. Tuscaloosa: University of Alabama
    Press.

West, R., & Turner, L.H. (2004). *Introducing communication theory: Analysis and*
    application, 2nd ed. NY: McGraw Hill Higher Education.

Wilson, G. L. *Groups in context: Leadership and participation in small groups,6th ed.*
    Madison, WI: McGraw-Hill Irwin.

Appendix A – Dialogs (For General Argumentative Analysis and Evaluation)

The following dialogs range in their degree of mindfulness and reasonableness from high to low. They are vignettes derived from actual conversational arguments. See them as argumentative slices of life. You are invited to analyze and appraise them to the best of your ability. If you wish to examine other dialogs, please do so after getting approval from your instructor. *Apart from assignments in an argumentation course, the dialogs are not to be reprinted or used without the permission of the author.*

I.

Manuela: What are you studying in college?
Chris: History and communication.

Manuela: Why would you waste your time studying anything but finance or accounting?
Chris: What is wrong with history and communication?

Manuela: You can't do anything with them.
Chris: I plan to teach.

Manuela: So, you don't want to make money?
Chris: How much do you want to make?

Manuela: Plenty!
Chris: How much is plenty?

Manuela: I plan on starting around $50,000 and moving up fast from there.
Chris: I wish you the best. Get rich quick if you like.

Terry: And, why don't you want to get rich and get rich quick?
Chris: I do but working in an office all day on finance and accounting is not the way I would do it.

Manuela: Why not?

Chris: I don't like calculations and math. The thought of spending thousands of hours of my life studying a major in finance and accounting to do more of this kind of stuff when I graduate just leaves me cold.

Manuela: Well, I like it. It's a challenge and fun, and it pays off big-time.
Chris: Then, you're going to be rich soon, and short of winning a lottery, I'm not. Can you afford to buy me an espresso now?

Manuela: Sure. Let's get some caffeine.
Chris: I'm with you

II.
Doctor: You have to lose weight.
Ricky: I eat hardly anything.

Doctor: your weight is dangerously high for your age.
Ricky: But I starve myself all the time.

Doctor: Let's restrict your fat grams.
Ricky: What does this mean? I'll pass out from lack of food.

Doctor: Eat no more than 15 grams of fat per day. That's reasonable isn't it?
Pat: I don't know. What can I eat?

Doctor: What do you eat now?
Ricky: Hot dogs, whole milk, walnuts, pancakes, white bread, and fried chicken mostly.

Doctor: Are you serious? All of these are very high in fat.
Ricky: I can't believe it. I eat hardly anything.

Doctor: Do you like all of these?

Ricky: I love them.

Doctor: OK. Try this. Eat only fat free hot dogs, skim milk, and multi-grain bread.
Ricky: I suppose I can do this. Anything else?

Doctor: Yes, have no more than two walnuts daily. Have pancakes no more than once a week and then only two light pancakes about four-inches in diameter. If you must eat fried chicken, limit it to twice a week and clean the skin before eating it. Also, have all the vegetable and fruits you like and drink no less than a liter of water per day and as much as four liters of water per day. Snack if you like on fruit or multigrain bread. Can you do it?
Ricky: I think so. I'll try.

Doctor: Try it for a month and then we'll check your weight. You might also try to eat nothing after 7 PM.
Ricky: Let's go for it. I want to be a size or more smaller than I am now. I'll go for it.

III.
Sundog: Will you come to church with me this Sunday?
Bobby: I doubt it.

Sundog: A little church-going won't kill you.
Bobby: God has never been very good to me and doesn't care much about me.

Sundog: You'd rather stay away from church and risk getting God angry?
Bobby: I'd rather not go to church. All these preachers want is my hard-earned dollars.

Sundog: You know that's not true. Why must you be so unreasonable?
Bobby: I think you're being unreasonable – spending your time in church, giving them your money, and mine!

Sundog: This church helps many needy families with our donations and you know it.
Bobby: We're needy. Has this church helped us?

Sundog: Oh, it's time for church. I'll see you later. I'll say a prayer for you.

Bobby: Well, maybe it will do me some good. In fact, say two prayers – one for me and one for yourself!

IV.

Teenager: I need a new car.

Parent: What's wrong with the one you have?

Teenager: It's old. It's rusted. It's an embarrassment!

Parent: It will build your character.

Teenager: The car sucks. It breaks down all the time, and I don't know what to do with it.

Parent: Why don't you take a class in automotive mechanics?

Teenager: Come on. Get real.

Parent: I'm serious.

Teenager: No, really. What kind of car can I get? I'm talking used car.

Parent: What do you want?

Teenager: I think a Firebird would do?

Parent: Oh, is that all? What price range?

Teenager: An old one is ok – as long as it runs and isn't rusted to death. Oh, say, $5,000.

Parent: Well, that's not a scary price, but where will you get the money?

Teenager: From you!

Parent: And who else? Do you plan to get a part-time job?

Teenager: Do I have to?

Parent: No, you can drive your current car.

Teenager: Okay, Okay! I'll get a part-time job and borrow money from Grandma.

Parent: Give me number please. How much is going to come from where? I'll kick in a thousand toward your, say, $5,000 car.

Teenager: That will help, great! I'll get $3,000 from Grandma because I have a thousand saved.

Parent: Sounds good. But, how will you repay Grandma?

Teenager: I'll pay her a hundred a month from my earnings from my part-time job.

Parent: Sounds like a plan.

Teenager: Let's go shopping!

V.

Snowbird: Why do you look so sad today?

Joey: Oh, my former lives bother me periodically.

Snowbird: What do you mean your "former lives?" Other roles you have played? Other conditions under which you have lived in your younger years?

Joey: No, I mean other incarnations I have had.

Snowbird: Do you mean you believe in reincarnation?

Joey: I wouldn't say "believe in." Rather, I know of these lives through direct experience and memory.

Snowbird: How so? I'm mystified and astonished. Never would I have guessed that you believe in reincarnation.

Joey: Why not?

Snowbird: Well, I just wouldn't have. You're an accountant, a Republican, a church-goer, a Viet Nam veteran. I just wouldn't have. Again, how did you get direct experience of former lives? I'm not saying I agree or think it's true, but I am curious. Would you tell me please.

Snowbird: Sure. I know is sounds strange at first. But, that's because you and I are Americans. Millions of people accept reincarnation. A very well known and respected believer in reincarnation is the Dalai Lama, right? And, what about General George Patton?

Snowbird: Yes, I see your point.
Joey: I took a workshop that taught me to regress to former lives.

Snowbird: Where did you take the workshop? Who offered it?
Joey: I took it in Toronto one weekend when I was visiting. It was offered by a guru visiting from Nepal.

Snowbird: No kidding? And, what did this guru teach you?
Joey: To identify former lives through meditative practice, a trance state, and hypnosis.

Snowbird: What did you find out? Who were you? Abe Lincoln? Mary Queen of Scots? Joan of Arc?
Joey: No famous people as far as I can tell. In fact, no names surfaced. But, gender, ethnicity, and role surfaced.

Snowbird: Let's have it. I'm listening.
Joey: In my immediate previous life, I was an Inuit woman and mother of three boys and two girls. I died at age 92 of a heart attack. That life taught me caring, nurturing, and compassion.

Snowbird: Sounds fantastic to me. Can you recall any others.
Joey: Sure, many, but I'll mention only one more. I was a British Lieutenant who fought against the Colonists in the American Revolutionary War. I killed many Colonists, was wounded in battle, but survived the war. When I was 53, I returned to England and was killed a week later by a thief in the night.

Snowbird: Well, I'm impressed, but I can't believe a word you have said. Can you prove any of this?
Joey: Not through science, my friend, not through science. Maybe someday you'll experience your former lives and then you won't think of me as being so strange.

Snowbird: Maybe, Joey, but you're strange in a good way.

Joey: Thanks, Tony.

VI.

Frankie (Native Spanish Speaker): I'm so sick of English and its stupidity.

Melody (Native English Speaker): What's the matter? What's stupid about it? It couldn't be any dumber than any other language, like Spanish!

Frankie: English has spelling problems galore that are unnecessary and stupid. Spanish spelling is easy, like German and Italian. English spelling is a nightmare and is foolish. Melody: You're talking trash.

Frankie: No, you're talking trash and being a fool.

Melody: You'd better make your point fast because I'm running out of patience.

Frankie: Okay. There are many ways English spelling could be improved. For example, all words ending in an "nt" sound could be spelled in one way with, say, "int" at the end - correspond<u>int</u>, pleas<u>int</u>, and so on. All words ending in an "ur" sound could be spelled with a "ur" ending – walk<u>ur</u>, play<u>ur,</u> trait<u>ur</u>, and so.

Melody: That's really stupid. I've never heard such an idiotic talk. Spanish isn't so easy to spell either, you know!

Frankie: Do you write or read Spanish?

Melody: No, but spelling's always hard.

Frankie: Not in Spanish, you clown. "Casa" is spelled as it sounds. Once you know the vowell sounds, it's easy most of the time, if not all the time. "Mesa" is easy. So is "alacran." It's just easy. English is spelling is just plain stupid, just like some English speakers.

Melody: I'm out of hear. Go back to Costa Rica or whatever Spanish country you come from, why don't you?

VII.

Spouse Iota: You're an immoral pig!

Spouse Omicron: You don't even go to church services and you call me immoral.

SI: You don't practice what you preach.
SO: And, how can you serve as my judge?

SI: You sleep around and then harass me about going to your church – a place where you meet future lovers.
SO: That's a filthy lie!

SI: Are you denying you sleep around?
SO: I certainly do deny sleeping around.

SI: Someone called me the other night and asked me to get out of your life because the two of your are lovers and have been together sexually for over three months after meeting at a church picnic just four months ago. Is this self-confessed lover lying?
SO: Mistaken and confused, I'd say.

SI: Must I give you the details I got from the love of your life?
SO: Let's change the subject. You're getting irrational.

SI: No, let's change our lives. Get out right now!
SO: Okay, I'm going. Good-bye. I'll talk with you when you're sensible.

SI: No, you'll talk with me through my attorney.

VIII.
Tetiana: You're such a typical Scorpio.
Lorenzo: What's that supposed to mean?

Tetiana: You're secretive, you hold a grudge, and you're preoccupied with sex.
Lorenzo: Does it matter to you that my birthday is in June, and I'm a Gemini?

Tetiana: That's not true. You're a Scorpio.

Lorenzo: If I show you my date of birth on my driver's license, will you believe me and correct your silly statements?

Tetiana: Let me see two pieces of ID.

Lorenzo: Just to shut you up, here are two. There, you see – June!

Tetiana: All I can say is that if you didn't falsify these Ids, you may be a Gemini but you act like a Scorpio

Lorenzo: What's the bottom line to all this nonsense?

Tetiana: I'm fed up with you.

Lorenzo: Well, there's the door. See you. Wouldn't want to be you. Have a good life!

Tetiana: So long and go dig a hole and jump into it.

IX.

Broadcaster: How long have you been writing news for radio, anyway?

Writer: About three years.

Broadcaster: Well, you haven't picked it up now, have you?

Writer: What's that supposed to mean?

Broadcaster: That means you're doing a lousy job.

Writer: A lousy job! You're a lousy reporter. Show me, if you can, what I'm not doing right.

Broadcaster: You're using words that might be suited for reporting in newspapers, not on radio. You're using words like "pusillanimous" instead of "cowardice." You're not using words people recognize.

Writer: So, you don't want our listeners to get smarter than they are now?

Broadcaster: I want them to understand me first.

Writer: Anything else?

Broadcaster: Yes, you combine too many words in a row that are hard to pronounce.

Writer: Such as?

Broadcaster: Such as the words "aluminum" and "linoleum" following one another in the same sentence. These are potential tongue-twisters.

Writer: Well, maybe you should study with a speech coach for awhile.

Broadcaster: Work with me, or I'll talk with the producer about finding another writer.

Writer: Are you threatening me?

Broadcaster: Just work with me. That's all. Good-day!

IX.

Nick: Alien creatures have been on Earth for centuries.

Sarah: You don't say.

Nick: Oh, you don't believe me. Well, they've been with us for centuries. They observe us and use us. Sometimes they mate with us to upgrade the gene pool.

Sarah: What do they look like? They must look like us if they mate with us without us knowing. Or, when they mate with us, do they sometimes cause freakish results?

Nick: Ah, there you go being sarcastic again. No one knows what they look like. They are like scientists from another galaxy who study us and help us along. We used to think of them as supernatural phenomena because of our technological ignorance 2,000 or more years ago. Now, we would understand some of their advanced technology.

Sarah: How can we tell they are with us or even mating with us? Maybe my partner and mate is an alien. How can I tell? How can I be sure? My mate behaves in strange ways around the full moon and in the spring. What do you have to say?

Nick: I say you're a hopeless skeptic. There is no way for sure that we can know of their presence, unless they want us to know, because they assume our form.

Sarah: Well, that settles it. My partner is an alien from outer space fore sure!

X.

Caring Person (CP): You're into trash, and I know it.

Person in Trouble (PIT): No, I'm not into trash.

CP: I know you're messing around with trash you shouldn't be messing around with.

PIT: What are you a psychic? Is this an episode from *The Profiler*? You don't know what you're talking about.

CP: If I didn't care about you, I'd let you trash yourself with all the trash you're involved with.

PIT: Who are you sources? Who is telling you what lies? I don't have to listen to this kind of talk. I'm clean and earning a straight living.

CP: You're dealing trash. That's what my sources say. And, I found trash in your apartment last week when I stayed overnight. I want you to be honest with me and confess to what you're dealing in.

PIT: You don't have a thing on me. What are you doing going around my apartment and digging for stuff that isn't even there? What are you dealing in? It sounds to me that you're too worried about me.

CP: I want whatever you're doing to stop. I want no more of it in your life.

PIT: You've got me all wrong. I'll check around to find out what you think I'm doing. Then, I'll get back to you. I'm clean. You got that! Clean.

CP: We'll see. You've got a month.

PIT: I'll show you. I'm straight and have been for more than five years now. Okay?

XI.

Jill: How long have you been eating flesh?

Jade: I beg your pardon.

Jill: I said, how long have you been eating flesh?

Jade: Do you mean things like hamburgers, hot dogs, steaks, buffalo wings, and so on?

Jill: That's right - flesh. Steaks and chicken are not vegetables, now, are they?

Jade: No, they are not. But, I object to your use of the word flesh. You're bad-mouthing the American way of life. In fact, the way of life of most people on the planet.

Jill: So, because the majority of people eat flesh, it's okay? Is that what you're saying?

Jade: Look. You must have missed a couple of night's sleep. I like meat, fish, and fowl; and, I'm going to eat it. If you don't like "flesh" in the form of ribs, chicken fingers, filet mignon, and so on, then eat your compost heap.

Jill: Oh, so look who's getting hot under the collar.

Jade: As some Dakota Indians I know say in a joking manner, and I agree with them, "Vegetarian is an Indian word for lousy hunter."

Jill: I've never heard such ignorance.

Jade: And I haven't heard such lunacy. Excuse me while I go have a double flesh-burger with cheese and tomatoes for lunch. Tonight, I think I'll go to B.F. Goodribs for an all-you-can-eat rib special. Now, if you don't mind, you're blocking my path.

Jill: Go chow down, cannibal! Just remember that in Korea and China, people eat dogs too. Maybe you should have your German Shepherd for lunch.

Jade: Go sit on a tomato! I'm out of here.

XII.

Marty: Technology drives me crazy, especially American technology. However, Europeans and Asians mess up too.

Yukio: What are you talking about?

Marty: I'm talking about how manufacturers keep changing the basic design of products even when they created a winning design.

Yukio: I'm not following you. Are you against change and progress?

Marty: Of course not! I'm in favor of improving things though, not just changing things.

Yukio: Well, that makes some sense to me. Can you be specific?

Marty: I sure can. Take the VW Bug, for instance. They stopped making the Bug in the late 70s. What morons! VW sold the world on the Bug's shape and utility and then took it off the market for the Rabbit – an embarrassment of a car. And, the dealers tried to sell the Rabbit on the grounds that it handled far better than the Bug.

Yukio: Okay, I remember what you're talking about. But, the Bug is back. What's your problem with that?

Marty: The problem, clown, is that VW lost the market to Honda, Nissan, and Toyota as a result of their stupid fiddling with a great little car. Get it?

Yukio: Maybe. Go on.

Marty: Then, as if it took a genius to figure it out, VW reintroduced the Bug with a bunch of worthwhile updates and also a high price, if I may add.

Yukio: So, this should make you happy. Right?

Marty: Well, sure, but it's too late now, isn't it? Besides, Toyota is now doing the same foolish stuff. The disease must be common. They had a great looking Celica and messed it up with changes several years ago. Also, they recently messed up the Camry. Again, changes, not improvements. Luckily, Nissan is showing greater wisdom. The Maximum, a car we like, keeps getting better without changing its look.

Yukio: Well, I see your point, I think.

Marty: You may not see my point, but you act on the point I'm making.

Yukio: How so?

Marty: What kind of a car have you recently purchased?

Yukio: A PT Cruiser, why?

Marty: And, what is a PT Cruiser, a brand new design?

Yukio: I see your point.

Marty: And, would you like Chrysler to change that design entirely or simply improve it?

Yukio: No, I want them to keep it the same for the most part and just improve mechanical and safety features. I like the car's appearance as it is.

Marty: There you go. I rest my case.

Yukio: We're going to have to get you a job selling classic cars, eh?

Appendix B – Reviewing Position Statements

Editorials and position statements present a side on an issue or answer a question a problem poses. Editorials and position statements can be utilized from a number of popular sources that are reputable in degree. You may draw opinion from articles and editorials in such newspapers as *The New York Times, The Globe and Mail, The Christian Science Monitor, The Chicago Tribune, The Wall Street Journal, The Financial Times,* and other newspapers as well as such magazines as *The New Yorker, Vital Speeches, Newsweek, Time, Book, The Atlantic Monthly,* and other magazines. You may use diverse newspaper and magazine sources for analysis, interpretation, criticism, or refutation. A list of 12 sample sources, reputable or otherwise, of editorials and position statements are provided below for your convenience and for illustrative purposes. You may seek out your own. Any of the provided sources are suitable for argumentative analysis. Again, you may wish to offer a counterargument to argumentative discourse taken from a source not listed.

Sample sources for editorials and position statements:

1. See the following excerpts from *Psychology (1993)* by psychologists Wade and Tavris [details in the recommended reading list listed earlier] on "Does Consciousness Need Altering?" "Can Lies Be 'Detected'?" "What Is Sexually 'Normal'?" "Intolerance and IQ," "Who Should Protect the Fetus," and "The Politics of Diagnosis." These excepts make cases pertaining to scientific knowledge. What do you think of any of these positions?

2. These two articles are from *Newsweek* (Fall/Winter, 2001): (1) Dr. Robert N. Butler makes a case for the myth of aging. Read "The Myth of Old Age"; (2) Gwenda Blair takes a stand on psychological interior in "The Many Faces I See." Offer your thoughts, if you wish, on either of these positions.

3. Mark Boal's article is from *Rolling Stone* (June 6, 2002) and is entitled "The Supreme Court vs. Teens." What is your reaction to this viewpoint?

4. Cathy A. Langemo provides us with a view of growing old in North Dakota. Her article is called "The growing (old) of America" and appeared in *Prairie News* (April, 2002). What are your thoughts on her article?

5. James L. Applegate, President of the National Communication Association (NCA), presented this speech which was printed in *Spectra* (January, 2002) as "2001 NCA Presidential Address." What is your reaction to the author's case?

6. You might choose to read and react to any of the following articles from *The Good News* (May/June, 2002): (1) "Who's Telling You What to Think?" by Jerold Aust; (2) "Should You Believe All the News You Hear?" by Jerold Aust and Scott Ashley; (3) "Mass Media and Bible Prophecy" by Howard Davis.

7. Consider this article from *Talk* (October, 2001) by Tom Shales entitled "The Culture Wars Are Over: TV Won." Where do you agree and disagree with the author?

8. You might consider evaluating the following views expressed in *High Plains Reader* (May 2, 2002) by Ed Raymond in his piece called "Wanna Buy a Dirty Picture?"

9. The viewpoint offered by Laura D'Andrea in *Business Week* (August 13, 2001) entitled "China: Under the Glare of the Olympic Torch" may give you grounds for reasoned reaction.

10. The article by Stephanie Woodard from *Mother Jones* (November/December, 2001) entitled "Olympic Windfall" will prove interesting. Where do you stand on what this author has to say?

11. This article by Sonja Rye Vadlid entitled "Searching for Voice in the Media" appeared in *Native Directions* (Spring, 2002). What is your response to what the author has to say?

12. This article is from *Book: The Magazine of the Reading Life* (July/August, 2001). The article is entitled "Ten People Who Decide What America Reads" and is written by Marla Abramson, Jennifer Clarson, Matthew Flamm, and Kristin Kloberdanz. Where do you agree and disagree with these authors.

Instructional Suggestions

Suggested Reflective Journal Requirements for a course in Argumentation

A journal of three pages with one entry per page is required. The journal should reflect on at least one of the argumentative dialogs listed in Appendix A. Two entries must be from your own observations of argumentation in action in your life directly, as you observe it in the lives of others around you, in fictional accounts in literature, and in mass mediated accounts. Your task is to take arguers to task. You should base your response on the criteria from Infante, which will follow soon, for analyzing and criticizing argumentation with respect to *content* and *relational* components. You may, of course, criticize instances of argumentation using all that you learn in this and related courses. One reason you are studying this material on argumentation is to become sanely and reasonably critical. So, you can demonstrate it in the reflective journal exercise.

Suggested peech Requirements for an Argumentation course: a speech structure might follow this form:

Introduction
1. Tell us what your topic is, why you picked it, and why it is controversial.
2. State the issue: for example, "Should North American consumers buy Toyota cars over the cars of competitors?"
3. Commit yourself to a thesis statement: for example, "North American consumers should buy Toyota cars over the cars of competitors."

Body
1. Present the main good reason in opposition to your thesis statement and document your sources. For example, other Japanese cars: Nissan or Mitsubishi.
2. Present another good reason in opposition to your thesis statement and document your sources. For example, VW or Audi cars.
3. Present up to a third good reason in opposition to your thesis statement and document your sources. For example, Ford or Chrysler cars.

4. Refute (prove false) reasons 1-3 through evidence, reasoning, and documentation of your sources. Show the weaknesses in the options to Toyota: other Japanese car manufacturers, German car manufacturers, and American car manufacturers.

5. Present your commitment to the thesis statement again: for example, "for buying Toyota vehicles over the vehicles of competitors."

6. Support your case positively with good evidence, statistics, authorities, consequences, reasoning, and any other means of legitimate argument. Of course, provide evidence that is taken from reliable sources you cite.

7. Show through good reasons that your case either obliterates those held by the opposition to your position or that your case provides an audience with a comparative advantage. [Note: The comparative advantage is frequently used in marketing, sales, advertising, public relations, law, and politics; it has the advantage of recognizing benefits in competitors that do not measure up to the benefits your position offers. For example, you might show limited respect for Nissan, VW, and Ford car manufacturers, but then demonstrate how your position to buy Toyota provides the buyer with the advantages of Toyota's competitors without their limitations.]

Closing Remarks
1. Conclude by reviewing what you presented in your introduction.
2. Summarize the weakness in the opposing positions and the strength in yours.
3. Link the introduction to your closing remarks.

The topic should be expressed in common language and plain style. If you pick a technical topic, such as methods of cataract surgery, you should explain your material and support your case in language clear to a broad audience. Since your instructor lacks omniscience and knows this, you should make your case clear to a general reader rather than to an audience of technical specialists. You must style your paper after speeches in print that present a case or argument. Your paper must address a broad yet intelligent and university audience; it may draw rhetorical elements from actual argumentative essays and speeches or from fictional argumentative scenes from movies (e.g., *Inherit the Wind*) and TV series (e.g., *Law and Order*).

The argumentative assignments are assessed on two fundamental grounds: (1) *content:* refutation of your opponents' position and construction of your own position attacking another's position or argument (the <u>content</u> component), and (2) *audience relations:* the interpersonal attitude and rapport you develop <u>through language</u> in your position paper (the *relational* component). The appraisal is borrowed from Dominic Infante (1988, pp. 45-54 and 69-80). For additional assistance on structuring your argumentation assignments, you may follow these guidelines from Infante in establishing the *content* and *relational* components of your assignments.

Content Component:

1. Summarize the opposing positions or arguments to be refuted.
2. Give an overview of your objections to the argument.
3. Attack the evidence presented in the argument.

   Is the evidence recent enough?

   Was enough evidence presented?

   Is the evidence from a reliable source?

   Is the evidence consistent with known facts?

   Can the evidence be interpreted in other ways?

   Is the evidence directly relevant to the claim?
4. Attack the reasoning presented in the argument.

   Were any important assumptions unproven?

   Were there inconsistencies in reasoning?

   Were arguments about cause valid?

   Were comparisons based on things that are not equal?

   Was reasoning from signs valid?

   Were emotional appeals used instead of sound reasoning?
5. Summarize your refutation.
6. Explain how your refutation weakens your opponent's position.

From Infante, you may follow these guidelines for managing the **relational** component of your position paper:

Relational Component:

1. Does the argument test and challenge <u>ideas</u> rather than people?
2. Are the principles of argumentation used with <u>compassion</u>?
3. Is the opposition's sense of <u>competence reaffirmed</u>?
4. Is the opposition allowed fair and reasonable <u>coverage</u> for what they are saying?
5. Do the arguers emphasize <u>equality</u>?
6. Do the arguers emphasize <u>shared</u> attitudes?
7. Do the arguers show they are <u>interested</u> in one another's views?
8. Do the arguers use a calm or somewhat <u>subdued style</u> of language?
9. Do the arguers <u>control</u> the pace of the argument?
10. Do the arguers allow the opposition to <u>save face</u>?

Insofar as you employ the following argumentative plan for developing a case presented by Infante, you may use the system to invent an argument in which you propose some plan in response to your commitment to a thesis statement and then support the proposal with reasoning and evidence. Remember that you have content and relational components to consider always. While the position paper must attack opposing positions, it must do so in a concise manner so that the stress can be on establishing your own positive position.

Your position paper may incorporate features from this form by responding to these questions:

1. A major issue may be stated as a debate (or discussion) question of fact, value, or policy [for example, "Should American homeland security be increased?" (debate question of policy); "What should the American policy on homeland security be?" (discussion question of policy)].

2. Problem

What are the signs of a problem?

What is the specific harm?

How widespread is the harm?

3. Blame

What causes the problem?

Is the present system at fault?

Should the present system be changed?

4. Solution

What are the best possible solutions?

Which solution best serves the problem?

5. Consequences

What good outcomes will result form the solution?

What bad outcomes will result from the solution?

Applying the Infante and related models of argumentation, you can add these questions to your argumentative analysis of content:

What assumptions do the authors make?

What has not been said? Concealed? Withheld?

What has been distorted or stated incorrectly? Lies?

What has been overstated and magnified? Knowingly? Unwittingly?

What has been understated and minimized? Deliberately? Accidentally?

Also, you can add these questions to your argumentative analysis of relations:

Is this an occasion suitable for argumentative relations?

Am I suited at this time (or at all) to argue with this person? And vice-versa?

Why should I risk arguing with this person here and now? And this person with me?

Who will gain (and who will lose) what if I (or we) choose to argue here and now?

On what level and in what manner can this person and I argue if I (or we) decide to argue here and now.

Topics and Issues Suggested for Controversial Presentations

Causation of events, health, sports, literature, exercise, diet, politics, ethics, clothes, religion, housing, economy, money, the press, film, law, crime, schooling, college, government, courts, travel, foreign language, nationalism, business, news coverage, sports coverage, TV "reality shows," TV programming, advertising, unions, recreation, art, restaurants, adolescents, tradition, feminism, education, style, fashion, competition, mass media, dining, foods, patriotism, police, military, hospitals, pollution, national security, Bill of Rights, chauvinism, alcohol, drugs, radio, television, virtual reality, foreign countries, transportation, careers, family, income, extraterrestrials, vegetarianism, God, and any other topics or issues that seem relevant to the purposes of instruction.

STUDY GUIDES FOR TESTS

Review Questions for Test 1

1. In what context in this document is argumentation treated?

2. Which argumentation orientation is borrowed from management theory?

3. Which disciplines does this author's approach to argumentation draw from?

4. What does it mean to be COCKY?

5. What does resistance have to do with preparing for argumentative conflict?

6. What power bases are to be considered in argumentation?

7. Why does argumentation concern itself with content and relational components in controversial communication?

8. Toward what does argumentation based on Rogerian principles strive?

9. What ideas does the term hegemony include?

10. Which terms are listed as complementary terms in a dialectical system of communication?

11. Which principles of parliamentary law, as presented by Alice Sturgis, are covered in this document?

12. What must prevail for success in parliamentary procedures, according to Sturgis?

13. According to Sturgis, what threatens success in parliamentary procedure?

14. What does Sturgis tell us must be done with actions that threaten success in parliamentary procedure?

15. What results in argumentation and dialectics when conflict is stressed to the exclusion of harmony? Should we look at conflict resolution and harmony restoration?

16. In this course on argumentation, how is argumentation described? A panacea? A special communication activity? An ethical act? A communicative act? Performed willingly – more or less?

17. Does this course aim to provide you with the opportunity for argumentation mastery or competence?

18. Under what conditions does your author say argumentation can be successful on a win-lose basis?

19. Where can we observe "hard" forms of argumentation?

20. What does dialectic involve, broadly speaking?

21. How do Makau and Marty explain argumentation?

22. How do Rieke and Sillars describe argumentation?

23. What are arguers supposed to fulfill in the mindful dialectic?

24. What does the mindful dialectic see as virtues and as vices?

25. What is the ideal in the mindful dialectic? What does an arguer do with respect to an opponent's powers and strengths?

26. Compare Eisenberg and Ilardo's argumentative continuum with the mindful dialectic? 27. Which term from their model comes closest to the mindful dialectic?

28. What is a proposition of policy, value, and fact? Can you identify and provide examples of all three?

29. How can we distinguish among open, closed, leading, and loaded questions? Can you identify and provide examples of all four types of questions?

30. How can we distinguish between debate and discussion questions? Can you identify and provide examples of each?

31. What does an extensional orientation to language rely on?

32. What is the difference between high and low levels of abstraction in words? Can you identify and provide examples of words with high and low levels of abstraction?

33. How have different types of definitions been defined: for example, dictionary, operational, and stipulative?

34. What is a signal verb, and can you give an example of one?

35. How can we distinguish between making a assertion using an noun and making an assertion using a verb?

36. What is sexist language? Can you give examples of sexist language?

37. What does Littlejohn have to say about feminist research and criticism?

38. What does "enfoldment" mean to Gearhart and feminists?

39. Explain what Sturgis means by a motion for informal consideration.

40. Which behaviors does Forni list as being the embodiment of civility?

41. According to Foss and Foss, what is meant by default rhetoric?

42. Which rhetoric, according to Foss and Foss, is default rhetoric? How Foss and Foss rank the default rhetorical options? Which is closest to their notion of invitational rhetoric and which is farthest?

43. What do Foss and Foss mean by an invitational rhetoric?

44. What do Makau and Monty mean by a deliberative community?

1. What purpose do premises serve in an argument?

2. Which questions do Engel's fallacies of relevance, presumption, and ambiguity answer?

3. To Toulmin, what are the meanings of these terms: claim, data, warrant, qualifier, backing, reservation?

4. According to Blond, what does the burden of proof include?

5. Provide examples for how to analyze consequences in order to build your case or attack a position advanced by another?

6. How would you distinguish a devil's advocate from an angel's advocate from a creative advocate?

7. Name argumentation success levels. What levels of fallacies are included in the argumentation success levels?

8. What are the ratios for argumentation success levels? List them: for example, what you are aware of vs. what you respond to successfully.

9. What are the argumentative strategies? For example, engagement, non-engagement (avoidance, evasion, etc).

10. What are some alternative channels of communication for arguing? How does each function?

11. As reasoned and reasonable discourse, what ethical bias does argumentation have?

12. During a job interview, what does DeVito advise with respect to BFOQ questions? To illegal and unethical questions? What are BFOQ questions?

13. What does Andrews advise to avoid a "rush to judgment?"

14. What are fallacies or fallacious arguments?

15. What do the following fallacies refer to (*nota bene* those in bold print): *argumentum ad vericundium*, arguing in a circle, fallacy of single causation, *argumentum ad populum*, fallacy of composition, fallacy of division, fallacy of hypostatization, *post hoc ergo propter hoc (post hoc* fallacy), fallacy of the straw man (person), *argumentum ad novarum, argumentum ad hominem,* fallacy of untouchable authority, fallacy of ambiguity, fallacy of presumption, fallacy of relevance, fallacy of equivocation, fallacy of accent, fallacy of amphiboly, either/or fallacy (false dilemma or bifurcation), fallacy of complex question, fallacy of complex question, fallacy of special pleading, fallacy of hasty generalization, fallacy of begging the question, fallacy of false cause, fallacy of the slippery slope, fallacy of false analogy, irrelevant thesis, *tu quoque*, genetic fallacy, poisoning the well fallacy, appeal

to ignorance fallacy, appeal to fear fallacy, appeal to authority fallacy, *fallacy of the average*, fallacy of the unknown base? You are invited to look up additional fallacies as well.

16. What is the attribution theory of conflict? What does it deal with?

17. Can you find what Toulmin calls the data, warrant, claim, and so on of an argument in the example presented by Matlon?

18. What does Mahoney have to say about the standard of a reasonable doubt and the standard of a preponderance of evidence?

19. What does Elder and Elder have to say about the various guidelines for assessing thinking? For example, "All reasoning leads somewhere or has implications and consequences?"

20. How do Elder and Elder explain each of the egocentric and pathological tendencies of the human mind? For example, egocentric memory and egocentric myopia?

21. What is the difference between ethical relativism and ethical legalism? Do these ethical positions have limitations? If so, what are the limitations?

22. What do Wade and Tavris have to say about critical thinking? Is there view negative only?

23. What does DeVito have to say about sexually harassing behaviors at work? Which behaviors are likely to be classified as sexually harassing?